Beyond

OUR

WALLS

Who would choose to live in a slum—with the threat of eviction, fire, sickness? And how does one live there and hope to somehow contribute to a life of flourishing? Rahma's story is one of honesty, reflection, and inspiration. She does not gloss over the hard times; she tells of finding the Jesus who emptied himself to come and live among us—the same Jesus who is present with those living on the rubbish dumps of the world, who share the little they have with generosity and hospitality. Rahma's story of living for a decade in the slums of Indonesia, invites us to take seriously God's compassion for the poor, and in so doing, to find life abundant.

IRENE ALEXANDER

Asian Theological Seminary and Honorary Research Fellow,
Trinity College, Queensland, Australia
Author, *Practicing the Presence of Jesus* and *How Relationships Work*

Kak Anita intentionally moved into the slums of Jakarta to unlearn much of how she thought life should be. In that unexpected context she met generous neighbors, fun loving children, concerned aunties, eager students—each with names and stories of their own. She also met, "Jesus in all his distressing disguises." Anita and her husband have found the courage and faith to continue on, together with their slum-dwelling community, in spite of demolition, fire, floods and various vermin and viruses. *Beyond Our Walls* is a powerful read, full of stories that inspire a deeper trust in Jesus, who lives outside the walls and invites us to follow him there.

ROBYNN BLISS

Co-author, *Expectations and Burnout*

While many of us begin well in our lives of following Jesus, very often "the worries of this life and the deceitfulness of wealth" (Mark 4:19) distract us, and before we know it, we are no different than those around us. In *Beyond our Walls*, we encounter Rahma. She is a modern-day saint, not because she doesn't make mistakes, get angry, or feel disheartened (she does all of those things), but because she has attempted to live out the love of Jesus for her neighbors, day after day, for more than a decade in a place that most Westerners would only want to visit for an hour. *Beyond Our Walls* is Rahma's compelling, funny, beautifully written, and heartfelt story. May it inspire us to continue on the narrow path, for all its trash and brokenness. For as Rahma beautifully shows us, it is on that path, beyond the walls, that life is found.

MARK DELANEY

International Coordinator, Servants to Asia's Urban Poor
Co-author, *Low Carbon and Loving It*

Over the course of Rahma's decade in the slums of Jakarta, the Word becomes flesh in the lives of her, her family, and her community. Now, in this extraordinary memoir, that flesh becomes words. Imagine if Katherine Boo and the makers of *Slumdog Millionaire* got together with Shane Claiborne and the ghost of Dorothy Day and wrote a book together, then you will have a sense of what you are about to experience when you open these pages.

PETER DULA
Professor of Religion and Culture, Eastern Mennonite University

Beyond Our Walls brilliantly immerses the reader in the stark, gritty day-to-day poverty of a Jakarta slum. Here you will learn cross-cultural mission from a radical practitioner, who dares to follow Jesus across many dividing walls, receiving and embodying God's tender, transforming love. You may well be won over by the beauty and extreme challenge in these pages to yourself venture over to the other side—where you risk experiencing abundant life in ways you could never imagine.

BOB EKBLAD
Co-founder, Tierra Nueva & The People's Seminary
Author, *Reading the Bible with the Damned, A New Christian Manifesto, Beautiful Gate,* and *Guerrilla Gospel*

This book is the poignant and painful story of a life lived in service to the urban poor. In these pages, you won't find simple answers or a three-step formula for reaching the world. But you will find the way of Jesus—simple, humble, and present with those who are downtrodden. Read this, and you will be inspired to move out of your comfort zone and find Christ in the slums.

CRAIG GREENFIELD
Founder, Alongsiders International
Author, *Subversive Jesus* and *Subversive Mission*

With the emergence of incarnational missions into the global slums in recent decades, idealism and reality need to be sisters. In this work, Rahma details multiple experiences of long years in the complexities of urban ministry. The stories are gripping, and Rahma's commitment impels one forward. Her account rings with the life of God in the chaos and tragedy of broken cities. The triumphs offer hope in what often seem to be impossible situations. Anita's story reveals an omniscient yet present God who is creating new history among the oppressed.

VIV GRIGG
Founder, MATUL program
Author, *Companion to the Poor, Cry of the Urban Poor,* and *The Postmodern City*

There are many reasons Christians around the world, including students and future missionaries, need to read this book. *Beyond Our Walls* provides a model of Christ-centered, holistic, cross-cultural mission in an extremely complex slum setting. It contains the life and stories of a gentle, strong missionary who embodies a depth of compassion, vulnerability, courage, and genuine love clearly derived from a Source greater than herself. Rahma's ability to weave together biblical insights and creative mission practices with painful personal experiences and the slum community's deep needs and strengths makes this a "test case" in mature mission integration. *Beyond Our Walls* exhorts and teaches, inspires and convicts, educates and enlightens, but never resorts to either sentimentality or self-aggrandizing drama.

MARY THIESSEN NATION
Affiliate Professor, Eastern Mennonite Seminary

This book tells the story of a young American missionary who moved into an Indonesian slum and tied her well-being to the well-being of her neighbors. Ten years later, Anita and her husband Yosiah are still there. Said another way, this is a book about costly love—a love so costly, some would deem it unwise. Yet Jesus embraced such reckless love, and I hope Anita's story will inspire you to do the same. In fact, this book should be required reading for all future missionaries.

JASON PORTERFIELD
Author, *Fight Like Jesus*

This book is not for an ordinary Christian who seeks comfort and success based on the American dream. This book is written to disturb our normal, lukewarm Christianity, and our false, materialistic sense of security. This book is written to call us back to our truest sense of humanity and dignity, where God, the Creator of the universe, incarnates himself in a human form and embodies the unconditional love within him. He loves us by coming as a man, who can feel, touch, and smell our deepest pain, sorrow, suffering, despair, and hopelessness. He welcomes us into a new life full of grace, love, hope, joy, peace, and freedom. Thank you, Rahma, for inviting us to follow Jesus into the slum to serve the brokenhearted, the marginalized, the neglected, and to live out the gospel of peace in everyday life. This work displays the spirituality of humility that Saint Benedict describes. Rahma's life embodies what mission is all about.

ANDIOS SANTOSO
Author, *Live Simply Leave Legacy*
Member, Mission Commission of the Mennonite World Conference

Beyond Our Walls is a powerful, wrenching, inspiring, and compelling book. Powerful because it is a mighty call to follow Jesus. Wrenching because it shows with painful clarity what it means to follow Jesus into the slums. Inspiring because Anita's and her husband's amazing faith shine through every page. Compelling because it draws us to live like Jesus no matter the cost. *Beyond Our Walls* is an amazing book that merits millions of readers. Highly recommended!

RONALD J. SIDER
Author, *Rich Christians in an Age of Hunger*
Distinguished Professor Emeritus of Theology, Holistic Ministry and Public Policy,
Palmer Seminary at Eastern University

This book reveals God's love in Jesus Christ through the life journey and ministry of Rahma, her husband, Yosiah, and their two children, among people in the slum areas near the city of Jakarta. They present the love, power, and wisdom of Jesus by their deeds and the simplicity of their lives. They live as a reflection of the incarnated Son of God. The impact of their lives and total dependence on God's power is incredible. This book should be read by church leaders and students in Bible colleges and seminaries around the world.

BINSEN SAMUEL SIDJABAT
Principal, Tiranus Bible Seminary, Bandung, Indonesia

Anita's stories have tugged at my heart for years, and I always appreciate her fresh perspective on Scripture. *Beyond Our Walls* details her journey of following Jesus into the slums — and letting him teach her how to stay there. Anita will make you think, and she will make you cry. Through her story, you will see Jesus more clearly.

ELIZABETH TROTTER
Co-Author, *Serving Well*
Editor-in-chief, A Life Overseas (missions website)

Beyond OUR WALLS

Finding Jesus in the Slums of Jakarta

ANITA RAHMA

WILLIAM CAREY PUBLISHING

Published by William Carey Publishing
10 W. Dry Creek Cir
Littleton, CO 80120 | www.missionbooks.org

William Carey Publishing is a ministry of Frontier Ventures
Pasadena, CA | www.frontierventures.org

Cover Designers: Fadli Simbolon and Mike Riester
Interior Designer: Mike Riester

ISBNs: 978-1-64508-448-8 (paperback)
        978-1-64508-450-1 (epub)

Printed Worldwide

26 25 24 23 22   1 2 3 4 5   IN

Library of Congress Control Number: 2022946758

To my parents,
Thank you for teaching me about Jesus,
And entrusting me to follow Him—
Even though that journey has led me
to the other side of the ocean from you.

A Blessing for You

I bless you not with something new,
But with something I see already growing in you.
May your open eyes continue to see Jesus all around you.
May your faith grow as you see God working in power.
May you continue to hold out the light
Which is hope to those in darkness.
May your humble feet always
Remember their beauty and insignificance.
And may the well of love within you never run dry.

Love, Sylvia[1]

---

1 A dear friend from my sending church wrote this prayer of blessing when I left home in
June 2010.

Contents

By Rev. Jim Wallis

This book is a memoir of Anita's experiences. All names have been changed. Throughout this set of very personal essays, the author quotes her personal diary, which she has kept regularly for many years. The whole book is really that—a personal memoir of faith and life—and one that I commend to you. I read this memoir during the horrible moments of Black Americans being massacred in their grocery store, followed ten days later by children being slaughtered in their Texas classrooms. Both incidences happened in the midst of the US Senate's inability to pass effective and literally life-saving programs for the poorest children and families in America. So Anita's reflections on "Following Jesus" and how to do so "Beyond Our Walls" came at a good time for me. This account is her story of following Jesus, beyond all the walls of our world, into the slums of Jakarta, Indonesia.

Anita comes from a North American Mennonite family whom I know and feel close to from some common work and history (I even helped marry her parents!). She decided to take the Jesus she learned about at home and at church to the places, both national and international, where she moved to live and work. She chose to learn more about who Jesus is, what he said, and how to find him among the poor and most marginal.

The remarkable stories in this book, about the mothers, fathers, kids, and all the new neighbors in the slums Anita deliberately moved into, reminded me again and again of my own conversion passage in Matthew 25 where Jesus says we will most clearly find him among the "least of these." This means that when Christians keep their distance from the poor and most vulnerable out of their own discomfort or fear, they are, in reality, distancing themselves from Christ. Anita's illuminating stories of all the people she has learned to love and who now love her, help us to see what that passage means in the slums and garbage dumps of the world where a billion of God's children live. Was her choice dramatic? Yes. Is every Christian called to the slums, as some of her best friends have asked her (and have asked her parents)? She says no, but she does ask all of us who claim to be Christians how and where we are following Jesus in relation to the poor—a practice Jesus clearly teaches as a test of our discipleship.

You will read honest writing here about Anita's own pilgrimage into the slums as a single, white American woman with the great privileges of an education, passport, and money available when needed for life, health, and emergencies. You will read about her meeting her Indonesian Mennonite husband (her mom told me she had to go all the way to Indonesia to marry another Mennonite, and might not have if she had stayed in America!), and about her giving birth and raising two boys, now six and eight, who in their slum neighborhood are surrounded by a community that loves and looks after them. You will read about how the lives and needs of those around her have led to all the work that she and her now partner Yosiah have begun with the teams of international volunteers and Indonesians who have come to join them.

It was their neighbors' needs, hopes, and dreams, that led this remarkable family to start House of Hope—a kindergarten and afterschool program right next-door to, and often spilling over into, their home. House of Hope prepares children for school who have never owned or seen a book. Or even had one read to them. For over a decade now, this little school, that now includes neighborhood mothers trained to be teachers, has sent these students into the public schools ahead of many of their peers. I have just heard that House of Hope graduates now have their first young woman alumna going to college! This story offers another proof that the best way out of poverty is educating children out of it. But, as Anita and Yosiah's stories also demonstrate, such a school wouldn't exist if these two college graduates had not decided to follow Jesus who called them to live with those in poverty. Additionally, Anita's extensive work with pregnant women, including everything from prenatal care through birthing and postnatal care, reveals both how much harder it is to bring life into the slums of the world and how new life is still the greatest human joy in all the world.

Again, this is not just a book about poverty or global development or education and maternal care—there are many other books about all of those opportunities. This is a faith memoir, which calls each of us to write or rewrite our own faith memoirs about how we are following Jesus into difficult situations. One of the greatest difficulties we face today is indeed the great walls between us. We are polarized by fear which leads to hate which leads to violence. These walls are the walls of race, class, and gender, which, according to Galatians 3:28, Christians should have the power to overcome. These divisions separate those who act like they are "white" Christians from the rest of God's wonderfully diverse children. These days, I find myself trying to *burrow through* those walls as the author here guides us to do.

This book is not a success story. The author, Anita, honestly, and sometimes with grim details, describes the utter poverty, addictions, rats, gender oppression, sickness, disease, and death of her neighbors in the Jakarta slum which has become her home. She speaks candidly of her own doubts and fears, of the sickness that struck her and her children, of the utter exhaustion and even despair, of second thoughts, and wondering where in the world she is and why. Her continual quotations of Scripture, both pertinent and powerful, reveal a human being of faith trying to find and continue her way forward.

Read this book and write, that is, live, your own continuing personal memoir of faith by following Jesus into the most difficult situations in the world today.

Rev. Jim Wallis
Inaugural Chair of Faith and Public Life, McCourt School of Public Policy
Founding Director, Center on Faith and Justice at Georgetown University

May 2022

By Scott Bessenecker

One night you have a dream in which you meet Jesus. After greeting you with an embrace, Jesus offers you a gift.

"Tomorrow I will allow you to see the world as it truly is. A world without the walls which separate rich from poor, marginalized from centered, powerful from vulnerable."

"That sounds fascinating," you tell him. "I've always wanted to see beyond my limited view of this middle-class world. To see it fully and completely, as you do."

"There is one drawback," Jesus tells you. "Once you see the world as it is, you will never be able to see it the same way again. Do you still want this gift?"

"Yes!" you say. "I want your eyes, Jesus. I want to see beyond the insulation of my small perspective."

The Lord bends down and pulls up a flower growing at his feet. He crushes it and an oily liquid drips onto his fingers. Then he reaches over to you and makes the sign of the cross over your eyes. At first everything becomes blurry, so you close your eyes tightly and open them again. When you do, you find you are back in your bedroom waking from the dream.

Your shower this morning is a simple bucket of water and a scoop. Afterwards, you head into the kitchen to prepare your breakfast. Your mother is there, seated at a plastic table on a concrete floor. You're baffled since she has her own two-bedroom condo in a nearby suburb.

"Mom, what are you doing here?"

"Don't be silly," she says, "I live in your garden shed. You know that! I live there along with your two aunties and their families." Then she coughs violently into a napkin. When she pulls it away, the napkin is speckled with blood.

Before you can express your concern, one of your aunts comes in from outside with a granddaughter on her hip. They are dressed in clothing unfit for a secondhand store.

"Is there a little rice for the baby before we head out to beg?" she asks.

"What do you mean, 'is there a little rice?' Of course. You can have whatever you want to eat. And what's this about begging?"

When you go to fetch food from your refrigerator, you see it is empty except for a can of soda. All the cupboards are practically empty. You find a bag of potato chips and hand it to your aunt with the soda.

"Here," you say. "I'll get some food after work and bring it home. And you shouldn't beg, Auntie. Uncle is working at a good job."

"Your uncle left long ago," she says. "And your cousin is very sick, so she can't go begging today. I'm going in her place with little Lucia."

Suddenly, you are not so certain that you want to see the world in this way. It's one thing to see strangers who live like this; it's another to see the family you love struggling in this sort of world.

"I better get to work," you tell them. You assure your aunt and your mother, "When I get home from work, we'll have a big dinner, and I will make a doctor's appointment for you, Mother. You need to have that cough checked out. I'm afraid you might have tuberculosis."

"Of course I do. But the doctor is too expensive, dear. We can't afford to go. Besides, I've gotten along this way for months. I'll be okay."

You step outside to head to work in this world without walls and notice your metal garden shed is open. You catch a glimpse of several cousins crouching inside over a Bunsen burner with a pot of water on top. A sewage ditch runs alongside the shed, and one cousin is squatting alongside it to do his business in the trench. There are dozens of garden sheds lining the trench. The middle-class homes which were there only yesterday are gone. A relative waves at you, smiling as you make your way down the dirt road toward work.

Down the road you come upon a palatial mansion with large iron gates around it and tall, ornate columns adorning a massive porch. You recognize a couple of relatives plodding away at the lawn and gardens. Two women are squatting outside the gates begging. Then the owner steps out of his massive home in a bathrobe to pick up the newspaper. He waves at you and returns inside. You can hear the snap of the deadbolt as he locks his door. It strikes you as obscene that one neighbor can live so lavishly as others beg at his gates.

You arrive at your workplace and see that it too has changed. The managers are well dressed and all of them are from the same ethnic group. Manager's offices are comfortable and air conditioned, but the rest of the employees work in hot, overcrowded conditions. Nearly all of the employees are from an ethnic group that has been historically oppressed, but those days are gone, aren't they?

That evening, you head home with two full bags of groceries for your family and some cough medicine for your mother, but when you get to your street it is impassable. There was a thunderstorm earlier that day and your neighborhood is flooded. You are at a loss as to how to proceed, but you see your neighbors walking in knee-deep water, carrying everything above their shoulders. Children are playing and laughing in the stagnant lake now sitting in the middle of your neighborhood. You hoist the groceries up above your head and wade in. The stench is strong, and as you get close to your home, you see that the sewage ditch has overflowed and wastewater is running through all the sheds. Nobody seems alarmed; they are simply moving about as if this isn't a disaster. You wonder what kinds of illnesses will start cropping up later this week as a result.

A cousin tells you that your mother and other relatives have gone to a field behind the shopping mall nearby where the ground is higher. They'll be fine with the tarps they took, he says. They'll wait until the water recedes to come back. It takes a couple of hours, but you make your way to them behind the mall and start a fire to cook some of the vegetables you picked up. Other neighbors are there too, under sheets of plastic or tarps in this make-shift settlement of displaced flood victims. The mall is a short distance away, and it is alive with people buying things that seemed like ordinary necessities yesterday, but appear today like extravagant luxuries as your family and neighbors huddle over cook fires in this nearby field. Some have foraged food from nearby woods, and others have scavenged from the mall garbage cans until they were shooed away by the mall police.

You drift off to sleep under the stars with your relatives and neighbors next to you. Relationally, there is beauty to this life, but that beauty is suffocated by disease, despair, and hardship. When you wake the next morning, back in the reality with walls that separate the world of slum communities from the world of suburban communities, you realize that Jesus was right. You can never again see the world as you did before.

~~~

I might have drafted a foreword to Anita Rahma's book, *Beyond Our Walls*, with a barrage of statistics that help draw a picture of the inequities of this world. I could have quoted from a variety of sources about the frightening growth of slum communities—exploding at three times the rate of global population growth. I might have listed data sets that expose the devastating lack of access to health care experienced by too many. I could have cited the breakneck pace at which income disparity is growing, or simply told you that between March 2020 and November 2021, the wealth of ten individuals grew by $15,000 per second. They were billionaires before the COVID-19 pandemic and they are trillionaires today. In that same period, 160 million more people were forced into poverty.

But I didn't do any of that. I chose instead to put you inside the global story of slum communities. The speed at which slums are growing is overwhelming governments who cannot keep pace with the demands for housing, jobs, or health care in these burgeoning shanty towns. But the wealth gap, poverty, poor housing, and health crises in slums are not driven by a lack of money or resources. They are driven by a lack of love; driven by thick walls that separate us from our brothers and sisters on the other side.

In *Beyond Our Walls*, Anita helps us dig our way through these walls to experience life on the other side. Jesus walks there among men and women made in his image whose dignity has been leeched away by empires built upon low wages and exploitation. She is learning how to live in this world made up of billions outside the purview of many of us. She invites us into the last twelve years of living in an Indonesian slum community.

Beauty and joy exist alongside crippling poverty and hopelessness, and Anita welcomes you and me to walk with her beyond the walls of our insular lives. In doing so, she helps us to see the world as it truly is. We can never see it quite the same way again.

SCOTT BESSENECKER
National Director of Global Engagement & Justice,
InterVarsity Christian Fellowship

May 2022

Wake Up

*Those of us who live inside the little Christian circle are
usually so engrossed by its many and pressing claims, that
we are hardly likely to see far beyond its borders...
God give us hearts that will care more, and eyes that are
clearer to see past the edge of the halo rim, over the walls of
our compounds, away up through His wide world, till we
feel as we never felt before the overwhelming enormousness
of the work that is not being done, in places where souls are
sitting in a darkness which does not pass.*
–Amy Carmichael, Overweights of Joy[1]

"*Sahur. Sahur.* Wake up and pray." The cries of young boys walking around
the neighborhood, banging on drums, wakes us around three o'clock each
morning during Ramadan.

It is Holy Week 2022 as I write these words. This year, Holy Week
seems especially unique, as it falls during the second week of the month
of Ramadan. Ramadan follows a lunar calendar, so the dates change each
year. This is the first time in my eleven years in Indonesia that Ramadan
has coincided with the Christian Holy Week, but apparently this happens
every thirty years or so. My Muslim neighbors fast from sunup until
sundown for thirty days. Many Christians around the world also engage in
different types of fasting in the days leading up to Good Friday and Easter.
As my neighbors fast and pray, I also lift my voice, interceding for our
community and my dear friends in this slum community. May God reveal
to us the *siratul mustaqim*,[2] the straight path.

I moved to Jakarta, Indonesia, as a young university graduate in
January 2011, bringing with me one suitcase, my guitar, and many dreams.
I had no idea what was in store for me, but I felt called to follow Jesus into
the slums. Was I naïve? Certainly. Was I brave? Perhaps. Was I foolish?
Maybe. Was I a saint? Definitely not.

---

1 Carmichael, *Overweights of Joy*.

2 *Siratul mustaqim* literally means "the straight path" and is part of the Muslim prayers
recited seventeen times a day. We pray that our neighbors would indeed find the One
who is the Way.

But I was following the One who calls me to march by a different drummer than the world. Jesus and his kingdom have captured my heart and my imagination, and I want to believe that Jesus has good news for the urban slums of today's world.

Now, more than a decade later, I am still here. I still believe that Jesus cares about the 1.4 billion people in our world who currently live in urban slum communities. Slums are no longer statistics to me—they are made up of real people who are deeply loved by God.

Along with my neighbors, I have watched our slum communities experience fires and floods. I have wept as children died of treatable diseases. I have seethed at the injustices of eviction and demolition. I have despaired at the cycles of broken families, interrupted education, and premature marriage. I have laughed with beautiful children who are my teachers. I have learned a new language and how to navigate different cultures, and I have been invited into hundreds of homes along the way.

Less than a year after moving to Jakarta, the slum area I lived in experienced a large fire and was eventually demolished. I reflected in a blog post at the time, "On the ruins of the homes of these thousands of evicted poor families, developers built a large shopping mall and apartment complex for the rich."[3] I am sure that no one who lives there now or shops in the mall is even aware of the story of devastation beneath their feet. Those who are comfortably renting these apartments or purchasing condos probably never think of the community that was displaced so that they could live there. Ironically, some of the security guards, maids, and janitors of these new facilities used to live in that slum. As they work long hours for the rich, they remember the stories from their demolished neighborhood.

While eviction was heart-breaking, the Lord graciously led me to start over in a new slum, which has now been my home for the past ten years. Along with my Indonesian husband and two boys, we continue to seek the shalom of the city in which the Lord has planted us.[4]

This week, as followers of Jesus around the world are remembering Christ's death and resurrection, I am struck by the following verse from Hebrews:

---

3 See Rahma's "Let Us Go to Him."

4 "But seek the welfare of the city where I have sent you into exile, and pray to the LORD on its behalf, for in its welfare you will find your welfare" (Jer 29:7).

Therefore Jesus also suffered *outside the city gate* in order to sanctify the people by his own blood. *Let us then go to him outside the camp and bear the abuse he endured.*[5] (Heb 13:12–13, emphasis added)

So let's go outside, where Jesus is, where the action is—not trying to be privileged insiders, but taking our share in the abuse of Jesus.[6] (Heb 13:13 MSG)

Each day, we have an invitation from the Lord to wake up and meet him, as he is present in seemingly forgotten slum communities—in the alleyways and shacks, amidst the stench of rotting garbage, rats, and flies.

It is my prayer that by sharing this story, you too will meet Jesus in the slums of Jakarta.

---

5 Or "willing to bear disgrace" (NIV) or to "bear the reproach" (ESV).

6 To read more reflections about this verse see Rahma, "Let Us Go to Him."

Breaking Down Walls

*For he is our peace; in his flesh he has made both groups
into one and has broken down the dividing wall, that is,
the hostility between us … that he might create in himself
one new humanity in place of the two, thus making peace.*
–Ephesians 2:14–15

"Watch your head," my friend called out to me as we hunched over to squeeze through a hole in the wall to carry in relief supplies after a fire in the slum community in 2011. Walls often surround slum communities, marking borders between "legal" land and "illegal" land. For those who dwell on the wrong side of the concrete dividing wall, life can be extremely difficult.

A major highway bordered this slum community, which was hidden behind a wall, with toy vendors and other shops along the side of the road. We parked the vehicle with supplies as close as we could and then carried pots and pans, blue plastic tarps, buckets, and other necessities through the wall. Because the hole was only four feet high, most people had to bend over to avoid getting a nasty bump on their heads.

This image of walking through a hole in the wall has stuck with me over the past decade. If we are content on "our side" of a wall, we will find ourselves driving past real opportunities of encountering Christ "in the least of these."[1]

Two thousand years ago, on the evening of the first Easter Sunday, the disciples hid in a house, heartbroken and dismayed after the events of Good Friday and the confusing reports from that morning. Even though the door to the room where they were gathered was locked, Jesus walked through their walls, stood among them, and spoke "peace" to them.[2] "Peace be with you," he said. And then he equipped them: "As the Father has sent me, so I send you … Receive the Holy Spirit" (John 20:21b–22). Jesus also

---

1 "Then he will answer them, 'Truly I tell you, just as you did not do it to one of the least of these, you did not do it to me'" (Matt 25:45).

2 "When it was evening on that day, the first day of the week, and the doors of the house where the disciples had met were locked for fear of the Jews, Jesus came and stood among them and said, 'Peace be with you'" (John 20:19).

told them, "You will receive power when the Holy Spirit has come upon you; and you will be my witnesses in Jerusalem, in all Judea and Samaria, and *to the ends of the earth*" (Acts 1:8, emphasis added).

Not much later, on the day of Pentecost, the disciples received the Holy Spirit, and the church movement was launched out of that room. The disciples were Jesus's witnesses, and the message of Jesus and the kingdom of God has since spread throughout the whole world.

But what if the disciples had decided to stay behind that locked door? What if their fear had kept them safely worshipping as a small community of Jesus-believers? What if they had not obeyed Jesus and left the safety of their walls? The world would surely look very different today!

My husband, Yosiah, and I occasionally find time to go bicycling around Jakarta. We pedal past fancy gated communities, concrete skyscrapers that seem to touch the clouds, and glamorous apartment complexes. Such wealth seems like a different world from the daily reality experienced by our friends in slum communities. We know that many of the city's wealthy elite are Christians, and we wonder what would change in this city—and in cities around the world—if followers of Jesus would dare to go beyond the physical, socio-economic, and religious walls that we have constructed to meet him in poorer communities.

Like Ezekiel, we may be called to dig through a wall—or to duck as we walk through a hole in a wall while carrying supplies.[3] Crossing to the other side of any wall is a lonely process. Those who do will likely be misunderstood and criticized by those around them. But as Paul wrote to the Ephesians, Christ is our peace, and "he has broken down the dividing wall" (Eph 2:14). As followers of Jesus, we must be willing to break through walls and seek Jesus beyond what is known and comfortable.

This quest to find Jesus on the other side of my walls of comfort and security brought me to the slums of Jakarta.

> What would change in cities around the world if followers of Jesus would dare to go beyond the physical, socio-economic, and religious walls that we have constructed?

---

3 For further reflections on walls, see Rahma, "Digging Through the Wall."

Chapter 1

The Art of Unlearning

Lord, as the Word you became flesh and blood,
And moved into the neighborhood.
Keep us from trying to take shortcuts in compassion.
Help us resist seeking quick, superficial results.
Please give us the grace to follow your downward mobility
And not just admire it. Amen.
–John Hayes[1]

In October 2010, just a few short months after graduating from university, I found myself in the Jakarta international airport for the first time. It was completely different from any international airport I had ever visited. Everyone seemed strangely subdued, and there was no music blaring over the loudspeakers. Even the architecture and art on the walls contributed to the quiet, museum-like atmosphere. As I waited in the customs line, I found myself making a mental list of the similarities and differences between my first glimpses of Indonesia and my previous experiences in the Philippines during high school.

I had joined Servants to Asia's Urban Poor a month after my graduation from university, and spent a few months training in Vancouver, Canada. "Servants" is an international network of Jesus following, justice loving people who live and serve among urban poor communities throughout Asia.[2] I initially encountered Servants in 2006 while attending Urbana.[3] As I heard Servants workers share about God's heart for the more than one billion people who live in slum communities around the world, I was inspired by their vision of inviting foreign missionaries to move into slum communities to seek Jesus's transformation. After listening to their presentation, I walked up to the Servants booth in the huge convention hall and asked, "How old do you have to be to join?"

---

1 John Hayes, "Incarnational Ministry."

2 Visit *servantsasia.org* to learn more.

3 InterVarsity Christian Fellowship hosts Urbana every three years. See *urbana.org* for more information.

The friendly person at the booth asked my age.

"Eighteen," I said.

"Well, then, you probably need to be at least twenty. Do a few more years of school, and then contact us."

I was frustrated by this answer, because I felt impatient and restless in America. The three years I spent living in the Philippines in high school left me itching for more.[4] But in time, I realized that God still had a lot to teach me.

Over the next three years of university, most of my learning did not take place in the classroom, but through my involvement with a church community that was trying to take Jesus's words about loving the poor seriously. They welcomed homeless people into their homes, journeyed alongside people struggling with addictions, and strove to make Scripture a central part of their community. My time with this church community helped me learn to love people struggling with poverty in my own country—an important step on my journey back to Asia. After many prayers and tears during my final year of university, I surrendered this beloved community to the Lord, recognizing that the Lord was calling me to take the next step on my journey of following him. I was no longer *running away* from something, but was *being called* somewhere. Though I had to sacrifice a place and people I loved, I embraced the journey ahead with joy, trusting that God was leading me.

In 2010, during my preparation time in Vancouver, I had assumed that the Lord would send me back to the Philippines. I had already spent three years there and was familiar with the culture, and I had been working hard at learning the Filipino language online. But through conversations with my Servants mentor and with different Servants teams, I felt drawn to visit the Jakarta team, as I had an interest in working in a Muslim context.

As I rode in a taxi through Jakarta—the capital city of the most densely inhabited island on earth, in the country with the world's largest Muslim population—scenes of dizzyingly tall skyscrapers, wildly weaving motorcycles, and dancing monkeys on chains flashed by my window. I saw glimpses of immense wealth and snatches of hidden poverty. Jakarta reminded me of Metro Manila, but on a much larger scale.

---

4 My parents served with Mennonite Central Committee (MCC). Looking back, I admire my parents' courage in moving three kids—ages five, twelve, and fourteen—across the world in the aftermath of September 11. Moving our family to the Philippines was my parents' way of living out an alternative response to the warfare that the United States government was waging as the solution to September 11. They wanted to demonstrate to their children that Jesus calls us to love our enemies, not bomb them. We spent three years in Metro Manila.

Over the three weeks that followed, I explored the slum community where the Servants team lived, and I spent many hours praying and conversing with teammates. I was discerning whether I would join them long-term. The team was made up of two couples, one toddler, and one single female. They were praying for another single female to join them. Was this the country the Lord was inviting me to serve in, with this group of people?

People always talk about what you learn by going somewhere new and meeting new people, but I was being invited to *unlearn* many of the things that had been ingrained in me since childhood. In twenty-first-century American culture, one ingrained truth is that we should be productive. As a result, we measure our self-worth by our achievements: good grades, higher education, or professional, high-salaried job.

In the slums of Jakarta, the Servants team invited me to *be* rather than try to achieve something, and to focus on *listening* to my Indonesian neighbors rather than doing something for them. This process of *unlearning* has been ongoing—and often painful. But over the years, I have begun to realize that my worth in God's eyes is *not* tied to how much I can accomplish in a day, but it is intrinsic to who I am as a beloved child of God. When I live from this sense of being beloved by God, I can respond with deeds of love. I have also had to *unlearn* the belief that my worth is attached to what I do. And I've had to *unlearn* my tendency to place myself on a pedestal of pride and pretend to be God. While work is good (and part of our calling by God), I can also pray, rest, and worship, because my worth is not determined by what I produce.

Entering this new country and culture as a learner, I had to reckon with my limitations: I did not speak the language; I did not know anything about the culture; and I most definitely did not understand life in a slum community. To approach these limitations as a learner, I had to become vulnerable and invite others to teach me, like a baby, for I could not speak and did not know how to survive by myself. I also needed to learn to "suffer kindness" by allowing the people around me to offer generous hospitality—even though I knew that they barely had enough money to put food on their own tables.

> People always talk about what you learn by going somewhere new and meeting new people, but I was being invited to unlearn many of the things that had been ingrained in me since childhood.

One evening, my teammate took me to visit an *ibu* (literally "mother," though the term can be used for any adult woman). This ibu was seventy years old, which is very old for people in Indonesia, and she lived in a room about the size of my aunt's laundry room. She had a sixteen-year-old grandson who lived with her, but since he studied at school across town, he was gone from five in the morning until eight in the evening.

As I sat in the tiny room of this seventy-year-old ibu, she kept giving me her peanuts and crackers. At first, I wanted to politely refuse her food, along with the food that other neighbors kept offering me. But then I thought of a phrase that I once heard, "suffer the kindness of strangers," and I realized that I am poor in many ways and have much to receive from these neighbors, who are so rich in generosity, kindness, strength, and resilience.

I fell in love with the people in the slum community, and my time with them was a gift, filled with joy. The three weeks went by too quickly, and I did not want to leave. I sensed God inviting me to return long-term so that I could continue to learn from the Indonesian people. I also sensed my need to *unlearn* many of the assumptions of my twenty-first-century American upbringing. Visiting this beautiful grandmother in her shack, I realized that she had much to teach me about God's kingdom—things I had never learned in my years of studying the Bible.

On my flight back to North America, where I would spend the Christmas holidays with my family before moving permanently to Indonesia, I made a humorous list of why I was glad to be moving to Jakarta rather than Manila. My top three reasons were: (1) No loud karaoke in slums; (2) stray cats are less scary than stray dogs; (3) Indonesian food is delicious!

In January 2011, I arrived at the hushed Jakarta airport for the second time; I was moving to my new home in Bandung where I would attend language school for two months before moving into the slum community with the rest of the Servants team. Instead of paying to rent my own apartment or house, my teammates found an Indonesian family to host me. I had my own room and bathroom but shared two meals a day with my host family. Living with a host family was an incredible way to learn, as it plunged me into the culture and gave me opportunities to practice the language in my daily life. My host mom and older sisters worked as maids in middle-class homes, and the men in the household were construction workers and motorcycle taxi drivers.

Local children became not only my best friends, but also my culture and language guides. The children did not judge me when I made mistakes, and they introduced me to many parts of Sundanese culture.[5] They welcomed me with grace and astounded me with their abundant love, always eager to pull me into their games. Whenever we walked somewhere, they asked to hold my hand, and I wondered if it was for my protection, or theirs? Was it to show off to the world, "here is my *bule* (pronounced "boo-lay," meaning "white-skinned foreigner") friend?" Or simply an act of friendship?

One day, they held my hand and guided me through winding alleyways to follow a circumcision parade. There were men on stilts dressed in vibrant costumes. Boys were lifted up high on a platform, decorated with colorful lion heads. Loud music blared as they processed down the street. This Sundanese tradition was a vivid reminder that I was living in a very different world.

I learned my numbers and colors from my nine-year-old host sister, who also taught me to play a Sundanese version of jacks. While her small hands grasped the smooth ocean shells confidently, their rounded forms were foreign to my hands. As I watched her lift two, then four, then ten shells from the tile floor with ease, I was humbled, no longer able to cling to my excuse of having small hands as the reason for my failure to excel at this game.

Her long black hair hung in layers against her shoulders and then cascaded down her back. She smiled at my continued awkward attempts to play, and I could see that she now felt comfortable with me around. I felt that I had found a new home, where roosters crowed at all hours of the day, cats fought on the corrugated metal roofs, spicy chili sauce was part of every meal, clothes were always hanging from lines in the courtyard below, and two-year-old neighbors called my name over and over again.

When Jesus tells his disciples to enter the kingdom like a child, I wondered if he was inviting me to blow bubbles, trust the children who were constantly expressing care to me, and laugh while smacking bouncy balls around. As I played with these children, they taught me how to be more creative and resourceful as they joined rubber bands together to make a high jump bar, turned discarded cardboard boxes into chairs, and transformed the common courtyard into a play marketplace.

In many ways, I was like a child—learning my numbers, colors, animals—and learning how to do simple things in new ways—hand-washing my laundry, trying new foods, using a toilet with water instead of

---

5 The Sundanese are the second largest ethnic group in Indonesia, second only to Javanese. Both ethnicities are from the island of Java but have unique languages and cultures.

toilet paper. In the midst of all my learning, I continued to catch amazing and surprising glimpses of the kingdom of God in this Muslim country.

During my first week after moving to Indonesia, I made a list of things that scared me: (1) boys who appear to be eight-years-old driving motorcycles, (2) little helmet-less kids on motorcycles, (3) my three-year-old host brother playing with matches, (4) children playing sports with straws in their mouths, (5) *krupuk*—a fried chip eaten with most meals (I am afraid to know how they make it because it is so delicious), and (6) the amount that men smoke.

Yet I also knew that as a Westerner preparing to move into a slum community, I needed to set my fears and judgements aside so that I would not slip into the pitfall of seeing my neighbors as "ignorant" or "impoverished" and begin to pity them. Pity is a passing feeling that does not change our hearts—we feel bad for a moment and then go right back to our comfortable lifestyles. Pity is also misplaced and condescending, because it distances us from people and blinds us to their inherent beauty. I knew from experience that the slums in my new home country were filled with beautiful, strong people who had endured hardship. Though they often had to face broken systems and heartbreaking circumstances, they did not need my pity.

Yet as a twenty-two-year-old bule living far from family and friends in this new culture, surrounded by a language in which I could barely communicate, I had so much to learn. I felt completely inadequate and doubted that I would ever be able to "serve" in an entirely Muslim slum community in Jakarta. As a bule, I represented all the painful history of colonization throughout Asia, along with globalization, Christianization, and various forms of cultural oppression. But I wanted to love the people here and to live among them with humility, empathy, and compassion. And so I asked God to help me trust that whatever good might come of me living in Indonesia would be entirely his doing. My prayer each day became, "Please Lord, grant me the grace to accept your grace for myself. You have already saved the world, so I do not need to. My job is to serve you, worship you, and love you. Help me share your love with others. Amen."

Chapter 2

A New Name

Pray also for me, so that when I speak, a message may be given to me to make known with boldness the mystery of the gospel, for which I am an ambassador in chains. Pray that I may declare it boldly, as I must speak.
–Ephesians 6:19–20

After a few months of language school, my host family accompanied me to the train station in March 2011. I was so grateful for everything they had taught me, and we all cried as we stood on the platform, hugging goodbye. They helped lug my ridiculously heavy suitcase onto the train, and suddenly I was in my seat, waving through yet another train window.

Riding trains always brings a smile to my face, transporting me to another time, before airplanes or cars became commonplace. Saying goodbye to my host family brought back memories of my train departure from Virginia, when I was setting off for Vancouver in June 2010. In the photos of our family taken before I boarded the train, I am holding a smiley-faced volleyball in place of my youngest brother, who was at summer camp and so couldn't see me off at the train station. Though we were all smiling in the picture, our eyes were sad as we parted. We did not know how long it would be before we met again.

When I joined Servants, I committed to a three-year first term, which my college friends thought was crazy. How could I know what I wanted to do for the next three years? I laughed and said it was not as intense as getting engaged and committing to marriage for the rest of one's life! Now, nine months later, I was finally moving into a slum to join the Servants team. Equipped with a small "magic notebook," which I carried everywhere to write down new words, my heart was open and ready to learn from my neighbors and from the Lord.

Over one billion people in our world today live in urban slums, and that number is rising daily. Slum communities, defined by the UN combine the following characteristics: "inadequate access to water, inadequate access

> Over one billion people in our world today live in urban slums, and that number is rising daily.

to sanitation and other infrastructure, poor structural quality of housing, overcrowding and insecure residential status."[1] As they say in Indonesia, slums are often built on "dark land," meaning residents do not have legal documentation for their homes. Slum communities are birthed as rural villagers join the world-wide migration to the cities in search of a better life. Land is purchased from those who claim ownership of it (in Jakarta, often just people who have lived there longer), but no legal paperwork is involved. Land may actually "belong" to a company or the government, and at any point residents of slum communities can be evicted and entire neighborhoods demolished overnight.

Various authors in the last few decades have written about slums, attempting to alert Christians to this global reality, and calling the church to respond. Viv Grigg,[2] Scott Bessenecker,[3] Craig Greenfield,[4] and Michael Duncan[5] have written excellent books explaining in detail the complex dimensions of slums and calling followers of Christ to not be blind to this global issue. It was time for me to not just read about slums in books, but to actually move into a slum community.

As I rode along on the train from Bandung to Jakarta, watching mountains and rice fields flash by my window, I prayed that Jesus would meet me in this new home and teach me by his Spirit what I needed to learn through my neighbors. I had grown up meeting Jesus in the church, but now I prayed that I would be able to meet Jesus in these people, in all of his distressing disguises.

When I finally moved into my new neighborhood in the slum, I spent hours walking around its tiny alleyways, visiting families, and meeting new people, eager to practice my language skills and learn about the culture. Everywhere I went, children would call out, *mampir* or *main* (literally translated, "come to the side" or "come play"). Each place I stopped, I would receive gracious hospitality from my hosts, who served me spicy new foods, tasty fried goodies, iced chocolate drinks, and sweet hot tea. Families who did not have money for shoes for their children heaped spoonful after spoonful of sugar into my cup, which overflowed with their kindness and generosity.

---

1 Baker, *Slum Life Rising*, 21.

2 See Grigg, *Cry of the Urban Poor.*

3 Bessenecker, *Living Mission.*

4 Greenfield, *Urban Halo.*

5 Duncan, *Costly Mission.*

> I had grown up meeting Jesus in the church, but now I prayed that I would be able to meet Jesus in these people, in all of his distressing disguises.

My vulnerability as a single female proved to be a gift, as many families adopted me as a daughter and sister and then began looking for ways to care for me and include me in family gatherings. Through these connections, I soon found a teenage girl to be my language tutor. She was grateful for the work, as she had dropped out of middle school because her family could not continue to pay for her uniforms and books, nor for the eye exam and glasses that she desperately needed in order to see the blackboard. Every evening, after walking about in the slum, I would sit in her house and work through my language book with her help. On my birthday, her mom cooked fifty boxes of special yellow rice for me to give out to our neighbors.

These were beautiful months. Every day I felt that I could communicate more, and I was befriending and receiving hospitality from the community. There were hard things, too—such as the rats scampering through the alleyways at night, the constant noise, and the pollution. I struggled with being the center of attention wherever I walked. And my heart was often heavy from seeing so many children living in conditions that seemed unfit for human habitation. But the beauty around me far surpassed the ugliness, and I had a strong sense of being where I was meant to be and learning what I was meant to learn.

One of the key things that drew me to Servants was their commitment to the principle of *incarnation.* I wanted to follow Jesus's example by moving into a neighborhood and living amongst the people I was hoping to serve. In my slum, this meant encountering all sorts of health issues, including the scabies that plagued the children. Mothers often attribute scabies itching to food allergies—specifically eggs—but I quickly learned to identify the bumps on fingers, wrists, and ankles. I had to learn to overcome my own aversion and be willing to sit on floor mattresses or cushions that likely had scabies or to hold little neighbor children who did. I also needed to be willing to get scabies myself (multiple times), along with many other sicknesses.

Our first year in the slum with Servants is supposed to be a bonding year, so we are not allowed to start any programs or "ministries." As a learner, I was to pray about how God might be inviting me to become involved in the future. During this season, I asked God to humble me so that I could practice the core Servants principle of *servanthood* and help others in whatever ways I could. I longed for *wholism,* another Servants principle, and prayed that I would have opportunities to proclaim the good news of Jesus through word and deed.

I wanted to embrace the Servants principle of simplicity so that I could live as much like my neighbors in the slum as possible. I shared a small rental house with my teammate, and we did without many of the modern comforts I had been used to prior to slum life. We washed our clothes by hand, slept on thin mattresses on the floor, and had very few possessions—mine were a suitcase, a guitar, and a backpack. We were choosing to live simply, stripping ourselves of the possessions that so easily entangle us, in order to free up our time, resources, and energy to bless our neighbors. Over the years, my relationship with the value of simplicity would change—especially after having my own children—but during those first months in the slum, I experienced a delight and freedom in traveling light.

Whenever I introduced myself to people in Jakarta, I noticed that they struggled to pronounce my name, Karissa (their attempts sounded too much like "crazy!"), and so I quickly began using my middle name, Anita. I had never been called by my middle name before, and so this was a new name for a new chapter in my life. But both my first name and my middle name have the same meaning: "grace."

One night, I had a dream in Bahasa Indonesian, which people say is a good sign in one's language learning journey. In my dream, I was standing in front of a class, and I was supposed to explain the meaning of my name, Anita—or "grace"—in Bahasa Indonesian. I settled on "a gift from someone—a gift that I do not deserve," though this seemed like an unsatisfactory definition.

The next morning, I remembered the grace-filled epiphany I'd had while looking over a train yard during a fall afternoon before leaving Vancouver: I do not have to live in a slum for God to love me!

My decision to live in this slum in Jakarta was an act of love and obedience to God's grace-filled invitation. I had not come out of obligation, but as a joyful *Yes!* in order to know more of his grace in my life. As I made my new home in the *kampung* (literally, "village," though it is used by Indonesians to refer to both rural and urban communities), the Lord continued to teach me about grace.

> We were choosing to live simply, stripping ourselves of the possessions that so easily entangle us, in order to free up our time, resources, and energy to bless our neighbors.

One day, I asked a five-year-old neighbor girl, "What are you doing?" This is a common greeting, much like we would say, "Good morning." She looked up at me and replied simply, *Lagi main duduk* ("I'm still *playing* sitting"). I laughed. What she meant was that she was completely bored and was just sitting, waiting for something to happen.

I often felt like this little girl—that my "job" during these months was to "play sitting" with my neighbors—but I was not bored at all! Language learning and culture learning made everything interesting to me.

Other days, instead of just "play sitting" with my neighbors, I helped them work, as I had discovered that this was a great way to learn new things about the community. One of my friends sold *rujak*, an Indonesian fruit salad. Once a week, I helped carry her basket of spicy-sweet sauce, fruit, and a knife around the neighborhood. Many people found it extremely amusing to see a *bule* selling fruit salad. Through this weekly endeavor, I gained access to all sorts of hidden alleyways and remote corners of the slum. Our team lived in a very large slum, which had many different "neighborhoods" and inner borders. Some parts of the slum were very dark—with shacks towering three stories high and narrow alleyways that only a motorcycle could pass through. Other parts of the slum felt spiritually dark because of the prevalence of gambling, prostitution, and drunkenness.

Sometimes the brokenness, dirt, stench, and darkness of the slum overwhelmed me. In these moments, I needed to remember the final Servants principle. I *was part of a community*. I was not a lone ranger, but part of a team. I was unspeakably blessed by my wonderful teammate and friend, Lisa, who had been part of the initial Jakarta team the year before I joined. Before moving into a slum, she had lived in another city in Indonesia for two years and could speak Bahasa Indonesian well. She was an invaluable guide and mentor to me, and we had many conversations and adventures together. In the evenings, we would sit on our second-floor tiny balcony and eat dinner, listening to the *Magrib* call to prayer echo across the mega-city around us.

Within a few months of my arrival, our team began to crumble as the two couples both decided to return to their home countries for a variety of personal reasons. Could Lisa and I survive as a team of two? Would Servants even allow us to continue as two single women? What was God doing, stripping away the team I had expected to "do life with" for many years to come?

In spite of my disappointment, I trusted that God had planted Lisa and me in this slum for a reason. If nothing else, I knew I still had so much to learn. As our team dissolved and our futures remained uncertain, I remembered the communion of peanuts and crackers in the beautiful and wise *ibu's* shack, my cups of overflowing tea, sweetened with spoonful after spoonful of sugar by my slum neighbors, and I sensed that God had been nourishing me through these meals, feeding me with Jesus's broken body. Remembering my earlier prayer that I would be able to meet Jesus in all of his distressing disguises, I wrote the following in my journal:

> This is Your Body.
>
> Your Body is broken, Lord.
>
> On street corners, holding out Your hand to receive small change from those who pass by without seeing.
>
> You are the children who board buses, playing small guitars and bellowing out songs.
>
> Your Body is broken, Lord, declaring Your love.
>
> You are plagued with scratched-open scabies sores, bleeding, itching all night long.
>
> You are sick with TB, measles. Your thin hair reveals malnutrition and is filled with lice.
>
> You drop out of elementary school. You work overseas in Saudi Arabia, spend your nights sleepless and your long workdays tired.
>
> Your Body is oh so broken, Lord, and sometimes painful to look at. But I'm called to love you.
>
> In Your brokenness, You declare resurrection.

Chapter 3

Taste and See

The angel of the LORD encamps around those who fear
him, and delivers them.
O taste and see that the LORD is good; happy are those
who take refuge in him.
O fear the LORD, you his holy ones, for those who fear him
have no want.
–Psalm 34:7–9

Lisa and I had a screen door on our house because we wanted to keep out flies, mosquitos, and rats. It was an anomaly, as most people just left their doors wide open all day. When we were home, we opened the main door to let the breeze come through the screen door—and as soon as we did, half a dozen kids would gather at the screen, yelling, "Accuse me! Accuse me!" (meaning, "excuse me"). This always made me laugh—should I "accuse them" of being incredibly cute, yet slightly annoying?

As I spent my days learning language and culture in the slum community, I clung to an image I had received during prayer while in Vancouver: a little street boy was holding out a piece of flatbread, offering it to me. In that little boy's piece of flatbread, I saw a beautifully decked-out table, laden with a feast. The words that came with this image were, "Taste and see that the LORD is good" (Ps 34:8).

Along with my daily experiences in the slum community, I was reading through a formation manual put together by the initial founders of our team, along with a variety of books. One article discussed the need for faith, hope, and love in pioneering a new team.

> To be part of a pioneering team often means sowing lots of seeds with little fruit at first. It seems all one does is sow seeds, yet there is nothing to reap from it. But hope reminds us to persevere. And the faith which undergirds such hope reminds us that we are not called to fruitfulness but to faithfulness.[1]

After reading that article, I wrote in my journal a new definition of hope: "Hope is believing that another reality is possible." I desperately wanted to

---

1 Porterfield, "Three Characteristics," 18.

believe in another possible reality for my friends and neighbors—where their physical needs were met, and they could know the love and forgiveness of God. I desperately needed hope to be restored in my personal life, too.

At the end of my preparation time in Vancouver in November 2010, I had packed my bags and headed "home" to Virginia before moving long-term to Jakarta, anticipating a restful, joyful month of celebrating precious time with my friends and family. But while I was home, one of my brothers, Paul (who is two-years younger than me), had a manic episode and was hospitalized and then diagnosed with bipolar disorder.

Also during that month, as I was riding in a car with one of my friends from college, she lost control due to the snow on the roads. Everything went into slow motion as her car spun in a circle on the four-lane road, and I braced myself for the moment we would go careening into a lamppost, tree, or another car. But the car stopped spinning, we took some deep breaths, and kept driving—thankful to be alive. This near-accident seemed like a metaphor for my life. With my brother in the psych ward, I felt like my life was spinning out of control, with no idea where our family was headed, bracing myself for the moment we would get smashed by a truck. Breathing deeply, I did the only thing I felt I could do, which was to pray.

My brother Paul had been my best friend since childhood. Although we bickered and fought, like most siblings, we became very close in high school and college. Watching his brain betray him was excruciating and shook me as nothing had before. They say that a manic episode is like your brain having a heart attack. My brother's illness felt like this—deathly serious—and our family sensed that our life together would never be the same.

After Paul was released from the hospital, he entered a dark depression as the doctors tried to work out the right levels of his medicines. He seemed drugged, unlike the brother I knew, the friend I'd always had. In this agonizing space, I struggled to discern whether or not to move to Jakarta as I'd planned. Ultimately, I decided to entrust my family to God and board the plane, but I carried this grief and weight during my first months in Indonesia.

> I desperately wanted to believe in another possible reality for my friends and neighbors—where their physical needs were met, and they could know the love and forgiveness of God.

As I prayed for faith, hope, and love in my slum community, I wanted to believe that another reality was possible for my neighbors—and also for my family back home. I wanted to believe that one day, the Lord would wipe away every tear from our eyes. I wanted to believe that one day, there would be complete restoration—a new heaven and a new earth.

As I prayed these promises for my neighbors in the slum and for my family back in Virginia, I thought often about a game my brother and I played when I visited him in the psych ward, which he called: "How Are You Going to Love Jesus in the Slums." The game was simple. He would repeat this question over and over again, while I had to come up with different answers. I don't remember my initial answers, but after living among my neighbors in the slums for several months, I had all sorts of answers for my brother. I loved Jesus by becoming a *kak* (older sister) to my neighbors. I loved Jesus by playing UNO and Dutch Blitz with them and having homemade pizza parties. I loved Jesus by welcoming twenty kids into my small home to color pictures. I loved Jesus by starting basic health education clubs, teaching older children to brush their teeth, wash their hands, and take worm medicine. I loved Jesus by fasting during Ramadan and hosting "breaking the fast" evenings with the women who lived close to me.

During Ramadan, Muslims are not supposed to eat or drink anything from sunup until sundown. In Indonesia, this means from around 4 a.m. until 6 p.m. In the slum community, Ramadan mornings started around 2 a.m., when children and youth walked around the alleyways, banging pots and pans and chanting, "*Sahur! Sahur!*" to wake people up so they could eat and drink before fasting began for the day. (*Sahur* literally means, "of the dawn," and refers to this meal that people eat when it is still dark, before fasting begins for the day.) The mosques across the city also joined in these cries.

Since it was my first time living in a Muslim community during Ramadan, I thought I would join in the fast in solidarity with my neighbors and as I fasted, I would also pray. While I had fasted from food before, I had never fasted from drinking water. In the tropical heat, I felt no hunger, only a powerful longing for water. I had never known such thirst before. The psalmist's cry took on a whole new meaning for me, "As a deer longs for flowing streams, so my soul longs for you, O God. My soul thirsts for God, for the living God" (Ps 42:1–2a).

During the month of Ramadan, I not only thirsted for water, but also for hope. I longed for more people to join our team. I longed for more Christians to care about the reality of urban slums. I longed for others to journey with me. I longed for *hope for my brother as he wrestled in the darkness of depression.*

I remembered my summer trip to Manila in 2009 with the Global Urban Trek[2] and how I had heard Jesus say, "Follow Me," through one of my Filipina sisters as we trudged through the muddy slum on the edge of Manila Bay. When we arrived at her home, her family had washed my feet. Now, two years later, I was seeking to follow Jesus into this Jakarta slum community, and I was learning to let God wash my feet through my neighbors. I realized that I had yet another answer for my brother's game: *I will love Jesus by allowing my neighbors to care for me.*

I reflected in my journal:

> I came here to see you in the hungry hands, reaching out to taste my freshly made bread. The parched throats gulping water after the bitterness of swallowing worm medicine. The feverish body of a teenage boy lying on the floor of his family's tiny room. The pregnant stranger on my doorstep. The prisoners shackled to five tenants and fear of what they know of You.
>
> But now I see my hands reaching for bowls of rice and spicy chili sauce. My empty glass being filled to overflowing with sweet tea, chocolate ice drink, hot sweetened condensed milk, coconut juice, and water. My feverish body being massaged by cool and gentle hands. My neighbor telling me to rest as I flop down on her bed for a nap. I am the stranger at the door, being invited into countless homes over and over again. I am the prisoner of Western wealth, perfection, and the need to accomplish something worthwhile. My neighbors are freeing me of these shackles, helping me to unlearn so that I can receive you, Jesus. And so this is us. The broken and the beautiful. The ragged and weary. The sinners and saints.[3]

I will love Jesus by allowing my neighbors to care for me.

---

2 The Global Urban Trek (referred to as "The Trek" for short) is a seven-week trip for university students interested in discerning a long-term call to serve in urban slum communities around the world.

3 Reflecting on who are "the least of these" mentioned in Matthew 25: the hungry, the thirsty, the stranger, the naked, the sick, and the prisoners.

Just as Jesus had his own feet washed with expensive perfume when Mary anointed him for burial—which he described as "a beautiful thing"—Jesus stooped and washed his disciples' feet a few days later. He *instructed them to serve one another in the same way,* and anointed them to face suffering, too. In the same way, Jesus was *teaching me to humble myself and live a life of sacrificial service for my neighbors.*

Chapter 4

Evil Tidings, Raging Fires

*We know we cannot bring the Kingdom and yet we are
committed to work for its coming. Living and working in
the sinful here and now, while believing in the coming of
the sinless Kingdom ..., we are being asked by God to be
obedient, not successful.*
–Bryant Meyers[1]

Seven months after moving into the slum, our neighborhood received
official-looking letters saying that we were all being evicted. "*Katanya,
mau digusur?*" I asked one family after another as I visited my neighbors in
their homes. *So people are saying that our community might be demolished.*
Evicted from our homes, from this land.

When I first joined Servants, I had known that I might face eviction
and demolition; these are commonplace realities for slum communities
around the world. But I was barely settled into my life in this community,
and so my imagination raced, wondering what demolition might mean for
Lisa and me and for our neighbors.

Would they use bulldozers or conscript poor men from a different
slum to force us out with hammers and brute force? Suddenly the vacant,
garbage-ridden field we walked through to go to the market felt eerie, as
I tried to imagine what it had looked like when it had housed a thousand
families. Three years from now, I asked myself, would my neighborhood
look like this field? Or would the company that was evicting us put up
some massive, fancy building right away?

"If we get evicted, I'm taking our front door with us," Lisa told me
one afternoon. I looked at the door, where dozens of children's handprints
formed the leaves of the tree. I smiled, remembering their curiosity as we
had painted their hands and smacked them on our front door. All those
handprints formed a visual reminder of friendship, laughter, afternoons
coloring and playing UNO, and the evenings we broke the Ramadan fast to
share delicious food. Lisa was right. If we moved, we would take our front
door with us.

---

[1] Myers, *Walking with the Poor*, 10.

I worried about how many families would be displaced—hundreds? thousands? This had been their home for years, some as long as a quarter century. Others had arrived only five years before. We were all squatting on borrowed land. There were no legal papers, no deeds of ownership, only tears, sweat, and memories of the life lived in this place. I realized that living in a squatter area dispels all illusions of being in control of your life, all notions of self-sufficiency and safety nets. Slum dwellers know that life is a fragile gift that can change in a moment. They *know* that they are needy.

> Slum dwellers know that life is a fragile gift that can change in a moment.

I also reflected on the way that living in a squatter community was sort of like a never-ending commemoration of the Feast of Tabernacles, when the people of Israel were supposed to move into temporary shelters (tents) for a week. God commanded the Israelites to keep this feast so that they would not forget that he had rescued them from Egypt and to remind them that they had wandered in the desert for forty years. The threat of demolition reminded me that my home was temporary—so were my possessions, and even my relationships. The little world I had set up with my day-to-day activities was all temporary.

Though this realization was difficult, I knew it was good, because I was learning to trust in God and *unlearning* self-sufficiency and control. During these tense months, I began to pray, "Lord, help us as we live in this wilderness, this place of exile. Help us as we long for Your kingdom to come. Come, Lord Jesus, come."

When I talked with my neighbors about eviction and demolition, they told me that they were more worried about a fire. Burning people out of their homes is an easy way to evict slum-dwellers and clear off the land. I remembered a silly game I had played with my friends as a child: "If there was a fire and you could only grab three things from your room, what three things would you save?" I never imagined that I would have to answer this silly childhood question in real life.

But then on Halloween night 2011, I woke up to the cries, "Fire! Fire! Fire in *Kampung B*! Stumbling about my house in the dark, I lit our morning prayer candle, noting the irony of using fire to see. By my prayer candlelight, I glanced around my room, knowing that if the fire reached this house, I would never see any of these things again. But my mind was focused on the raging fire outside, destroying homes and possessions and possibly taking lives.

Lord, have mercy upon us. *Tuhan, kasihani kami.*

I quickly stuffed my hymnal, Bible, concordance, and journal into my backpack, along with the Mother Teresa daily quote calendar that my grandfather had given me. Then I added my Filipino sarung and a pillowcase made by a dear friend from college. In my other hand, I grabbed my guitar. With a last look around my room, I blew out the candle and carefully walked down the wooden stairs in the dark.

As I walked into the alleyway, I could see the billowing flames in the distance, women pulling their crying children away from the fire, followed by men carrying huge bundles on their backs.

After storing my guitar and backpack at a friend's house in a nearby neighborhood, I returned to watch the fire and see if any of my neighbors needed help. Masses of people filled the alleyways, holding children and bags of clothing. I saw four girls and a mother huddled together in a corner, and as soon as they called out to me, I recognized them from my neighborhood. "We lost everything," the mom told me. "We only have the clothes on our backs."

We embraced one another and sat down together on the side of the road. The one-year-old was asleep in a cloth wrapped around her mother. The three-year-old and four-year-old held hands tightly, wide-eyed and silent. The thirteen-year-old girl was watchfully alert, as if guarding her mom and siblings. I knew there were six more children in this family and prayed that they were safe.

After a while, I got up and went to search for other friends. As I passed one of my adoptive family's houses, they scolded me for wandering toward the fire and made me sit down with them on their doorstep, then gave me a cup of water. Eventually, the raging fire began to settle. We watched the firefighters spray the flames and then, at last, the coals.

After thanking my family for the water and companionship, I moved through the swirling ash and smoke, praying with the psalmist over and over again. "The LORD is my shepherd. I shall not want … Even though I walk through the darkest valley, I fear no evil, for you are with me; your rod and your staff—they comfort me" (Ps 23:1, 4). Though I had been part of this community for over half a year, I still felt acutely like an outsider.

When I returned to my rental house, which had not been touched by the fire, I found all my possessions intact. The past three hours suddenly seemed like a dream. After placing my books on the little shelves, the pillowcase on my bed, and my guitar in the corner, it seemed as if nothing had changed. But I knew that everything had changed for hundreds of my neighbors, and I wept as I tried to quiet my racing mind so that I could fall asleep.

The next morning, I walked through the neighborhood and saw the devastation: Kampung B lay in ashes, with little evidence of the homes that had been flattened by the fire. All that remained was the skeleton of the community toilets, the *Musholla* (small mosque), and one house.

The mountain of trash on the edge of the community had been turned into temporary housing for the victims of the fire. As I moved toward the large blue plastic tents that had been set up on top of the garbage, a close friend came walking toward me. Her head was draped in beautiful brown batik fabric to shield her from the hot sun. "It's gone. Our house is gone," she said without tears. "Kampung B is in ashes."

One purposeful strike of a match, one intentional flick of the bribed arsonist's lighter had brought about this ruin and the tears of so many children—leaving hundreds homeless and thousands afraid.

"The love of money is a root of all kinds of evils!" (1 Tim 6:10 ESV). A man's love of a bribe. The company's love of money—desiring the land that is theirs on paper but in actuality has been tamed and inhabited for over a decade by these people. The love of money reduces human beings to obstacles, to numbers, to obstructions. It reduces human pain to a necessary causality. It blinds. It treats humans like animals to be burnt out of holes.

Later that week, a sweet little girl whose house had burned down told me, "It's lucky your house didn't burn down, so we can still come here and learn about health and color pictures." Like so many of my neighbors, this little girl was teaching me about God's kingdom. *Rather than finding security in owning their own homes—or having cars, college degrees, health insurance, and savings accounts—my slum-dwelling friends were showing me how to become completely dependent on God's mercy to survive each and every day.*

The love of money reduces human beings to obstacles, to numbers, to obstructions. It reduces human pain to a necessary causality.

Chapter 5

The Miracle House

But now thus says the LORD,
he who created you, O Jacob, he who formed you, O Israel:
Do not fear, for I have redeemed you;
I have called you by name, you are mine.
When you pass through the waters, I will be with you;
and through the rivers, they shall not overwhelm you;
when you walk through fire you shall not be burned,
and the flame shall not consume you.
–Isaiah 43:1–2

After the fire, Lisa and I tried to ask our neighbors questions about how we might help instead of assuming that we could anticipate what they needed after losing their homes and all their possessions. To each of our friends, we asked, "What is the most important thing you need right now?"

One common answer surprised me: "School uniforms and shoes."

These items would have been low on my list of things to provide after a fire, but the parents in the community knew that uniforms and shoes were immediately necessary so that their children would not have to miss school. So we bought one set of school uniforms and new shoes for each of the school children affected by the fire.

After school uniforms, we provided other things suggested by the community: small cooking stoves, basic cooking pots, buckets for washing laundry, and large blue tarps so that they could erect tents over the ashes of their homes.

Jakarta's rainy season had just started, and I knew the rains would make daily life even more miserable for the families who had lost their homes and were living under plastic tarps. Though I have always loved the sound of tropical rainstorms, after living in a slum, I have realized that many people's houses leak; the frequent flooding disrupts their livelihoods, making life even more difficult. But I have many significant memories of rainstorms during my childhood, and the sound of heavy rain still takes me back to age twelve, when my family was visiting a rainforest in Honduras. I woke up in the middle of the night, and the electricity was out, and I had to crawl to the bathroom in the dark, surrounded by the deafening roar of the rain. Pounding rain takes me back to getting sopping wet playing volleyball with my brothers in the street in front of our house in the Philippines. Torrential rain takes me back to the day one of my high school classmates died of anorexia, and my friends and I mourned by playing tennis during a downpour. Monsoon rains take me back to the summer I was visiting the Philippines, watching trash flow through the canals in the slum community with my host sisters. But once I moved into a slum, the rainy season was no longer as pleasant.

> I was also longing for the Christians who were sitting in the pews next to me to meet Jesus amongst my currently homeless friends, who were cooking meat on top of the trash mountain.

Several days after the fire, Muslims celebrated the second largest Islamic holiday of the year, Idul Adha. This holiday commemorates the story of God providing an animal sacrifice so that Abraham would not have to sacrifice his son. During Idul Adha, those who have money purchase goats, sheep, or cows to donate to mosques as a sacrifice. The sacrificial meat is then distributed to the poor. I will never forget that particular Idul Adha, watching my friends who had lost everything in the fire joyfully cooking the meat that they had received on their little stoves on top of the trash mountain.

Idul Adha also happened to fall on a Sunday that year. During communion at my church that morning, as I took the little glass of grape juice and the little white wafer, I began to cry as I remembered Jesus's sacrifice and longed for my neighbors to know him as the "sacrificial lamb" provided by God. But at the same time, I was also longing for the Christians who were sitting in the pews next to me to meet Jesus amongst my currently homeless friends, who were cooking meat on top of the trash mountain.

As I sat in the pew, aching with these longings, I saw an image of Jesus hanging on the cross on top of the mountain of trash, his blood flowing down the hill into the dirty, trash-filled canals. As I prayed for Jesus's blood to bring healing and restoration to all the people living there, I felt Jesus inviting me to continue to meet him in the neighborhood around the trash mountain.

In the weeks following the fire, the community began to rebuild itself. Some people emptied their meager savings to buy materials to rebuild their homes. Others got loans—the lucky ones from family members, the rest from exploitative loan sharks. Before the fire, most of the homes had been constructed out of corrugated metal scraps, drywall, plywood, and cardboard—all crudely and haphazardly fastened together. This time, people rebuilt with cinder blocks. Block by block, the community began to rise up from the ashes.

The only house that had not burned down in the area destroyed by the fire began to be called *Rumah Ajaib* ("The Miracle House"). As I helped with fire relief in this part of the slum each day, I felt more and more drawn to move to this section of the slum. As I passed by the Miracle House each day, I noticed that it was vacant and felt it would be a perfect little home. After talking with neighbors, who introduced me to the landlord's relatives, I offered to rent the Miracle House. It was tiny—129 square feet (three by four meters)—and had its own bathroom, but no running water. Though I felt a little bit scared to live on my own, I believed that God was inviting me to trust him as I sought to meet Jesus in that part of the slum.

Since I didn't have running water, I learned to wash my clothes at the communal water spigot, where I met and talked with other women who lived nearby. I also filled buckets of water at the spigot and carried them to my house for washing myself and my dishes.

"*Kak, belajar Tomat, dong!*" four-year-old Andini called from my doorstep one day. ("Older Sister, let's learn Tomato!") What she meant was, "Let's read *Veggie Tales*." I smiled as I looked at her little face, which was pressed up against my screen.

Shortly after moving into the Miracle House, I had begun to read *Veggie Tales* stories with the children I was getting to know in the neighborhood. Day after day, we learned counting (how many veggies are in the boat with Bob the Tomato?), shapes (Pa Grape creates different shaped tires for his car), and colors (Junior Asparagus taught us). On Saturday afternoons, my tiny home became a movie theater for thirty children, as we watched singing vegetables tell silly stories together. I have sometimes wondered if I am the only person to introduce *Veggie Tales* to Indonesian Muslim slum children!

As these children came to my house to read these books and also color, play cards, sing songs, bake cookies and pizza, and receive Neosporin for their scraped knees, I began to fall in love with them—and to be loved by them and receive God's love through them. When I walked through the community each day, I would hear countless children calling, "*kak, kak*" (older sister) after me.

On Monday nights, five friends from the church I attended started coming to play with the children in my tiny Miracle House. As I watched my friends begin to love—and be loved by—these children, I thought of Jesus instructing his disciples, "Let the little children come to me, and do not stop them; for it is to such as these that the kingdom of heaven belongs" (Matt 19:14).

"*Terima kasih Tuhan, Kau ciptakanku,*" Andini sang on my doorstep. ("Thank you, Lord, for creating me!") Dancing from one foot to the other, she repeated this line from a song we had taught her over and over again, her curly short hair bobbing up and down. Pressing her face against the screen, she called, "*Kak, belajar Tomat, dong!*" ("Let's learn Tomato"). I smiled, reached for the *Veggie Tales* book, and pushed open the screen door.

But that smile did not stay on my face for long, as I saw the signs of impending demolition bearing down on our little community.

Though it would take weeks for this tidal wave to reach us, we knew our neighborhood would soon be swallowed and spit back out. Unlike a tidal wave, however, fellow slum dwellers would wreak this devastation—cutting down trees, swinging hammers into walls, tearing off roofs and doors, breaking windows, reducing each carefully constructed house to a heap of rubble, turning hundreds of neighbors onto the streets. We knew the fate awaiting us, because we could see the destruction in adjacent sections of the slum, where everyone had already been evicted.

> I thought of Jesus instructing his disciples, "Let the little children come to me, and do not stop them; for it is to such as these that the kingdom of heaven belongs" (Matt 19:14).

All that remained of these once vibrant neighborhoods were random clues of the people that had lived there: stray sandals, broken chairs, stuffed animals half-buried in mud. The ghosts of this wreckage cried out, *hundreds of families once lived here.*

Then we began to watch house by house disappear in our own area of the slum, evidence that the tenants had claimed their small recompense money and left during the night to avoid judgement from their neighbors. Renters received the equivalent of a month's rent as eviction compensation ($50), and home owners received arbitrary amounts, normally under $500. Each demolished house left a gaping hole in the neighborhood and reminded me of an infected mouth—one tooth disappearing after another. Children made playgrounds out of the ruins, climbing to the top of a pile of debris and jumping to the ground, digging for treasures, and exploring the shell of a partially destroyed shack.

Shortly before my landlord finally decided to claim his compensation money and tear down the Miracle House, I gathered with dozens of children in my tiny room. As we clapped our hands and did the hokey pokey, I wondered how many more nights there would be to play together before we were all scattered. I prayed that someone would step in to stop the destruction, but I braced myself for what seemed inevitable.

Then in March 2012, only four short months after I moved into the Miracle House, the "time to tear down" arrived (Eccl 3:3). I understood that there were countless other slums where I could live, and I knew that they would all have hundreds of other children for me to love—and who would love me. But I would miss each of these kids, whom I knew by name—not as statistics, but as individual children with stories that were still being written, dreams that were still unfolding, beautiful smiles lighting up their distinctive eyes, and unique laughs.

Terima Kasih, Tuhan, Kau ciptakan mereka. (Thank you, Lord, for creating them.) Amen.

Chapter 6

Out of the Rubble

*And I will appoint a place for my people Israel and will
plant them, so that they may live in their own place, and
be disturbed no more; and evildoers shall afflict them no
more ... and I will give you rest from all your enemies.
Moreover the LORD declares to you that the LORD will
make you a house.*
–2 Samuel 7:10–11

When the appointed demolition day arrived, I stood in front of my little
Miracle House and watched men from the community climb onto the
roof and start throwing the clay tiles onto the ground. Shards of clay flew
everywhere.

As I pushed a cartload of belongings down the walkway, I watched a
man chop down the little plumeria tree that I had planted in front of the
house only a few months before. Devastated, I put my head down and kept
pushing my cart of possessions down the alleyway towards my teammate
Lisa's new house.[1]

When I turned the corner at the end of our alleyway, I saw my ten-
year-old friend, Gusti, whose house had not yet been destroyed. I sat down
next to him on the pavement and asked, "Which makes you sadder: the
fire or the demolition?" He picked up a piece of broken cement block and
said, "The demolition." He threw the cement piece at the ruin of a house
and said, "Dini." Then picking up several pieces of cement, he threw one
after another at a different house, naming the friend who had lived there:
"Agus, Ramadan, Bagas ... It is so empty here now."

Some of the families who had been evicted had moved back home to
their ancestral villages, while others had rented small homes in nearby
"legal" neighborhoods. Others searched for land where they could rebuild

---

1 Lisa and I initially received eviction letters in October 2011, along with that particular
section of the slum. At the end of November, Lisa moved to a new rental home outside
the area being threatened with eviction and I moved into the Miracle House, knowing
that eviction would inevitably come. When the Miracle House got demolished, Lisa
graciously let me sleep on the floor of her little house, while I prayed and discerned what
my next steps should be.

and start afresh. Several days after moving out of the Miracle House, I accompanied four moms to survey a new slum community on the edge of Jakarta. We rode public transportation for an hour and then walked with excitement into the area where we might make a new home.

The community was still very new and did not have paved roads. Since it was the rainy season, we had to take our sandals off so we could trudge through the ankle-deep mud to avoid losing our sandals and having to return barefoot. Tall grass grew on either side of the road, and I felt as if we were entering a rural village. This area was so different from our inner-city slum—I wondered if God could be calling me to such a place.

Over the next several weeks, about fifty families from our old slum decided to relocate to this new community. The land was cheap, and they could start over, but they would have the familiarity and security of some long-term friendships. I was very glad when they invited me to join them and decided to buy two plots of land next to my best friend's family, which cost two hundred dollars for fifty square meters (538 square feet). On one plot, I would build a house, and the other was for future dreaming—perhaps a community center or school? We bought the land from a shady "middle-man," who claimed to work for the company who owned the land. For a few years afterwards, every resident of the slum had to pay monthly security fees to this middle-man. Eventually, he got kicked out and was never seen again.

Building a new house and relocating to a new slum were not the only surprising things in my life during this time. The Lord had called a young Indonesian man to our team. I had met Yosiah at the Mennonite church we were both attending, and he had visited the old community a few months before the fire with the young adult group from our church. Following the fire, Yosiah had skipped work for the week and helped with fire relief, driving the church's old white car to help purchase and deliver the fire response items. During this time, he felt God inviting him, saying, "*I am present here with these people who have just lost everything in the fire. Would you like to come learn from me in this place, too?*"

Yosiah was a college graduate and had a good day job. But after work each day in November 2011, he faithfully began coming to the community to help with the children's club in my house. He also began teaching guitar to interested youth. As he saw the reality of this different Jakarta, the Lord began to break his heart. Over the next several months, we began to realize that our stories were combining—that God could use us together to serve in a slum. His joyful spirit and personality began to brighten up my life in ways I never could have imagined. I no longer had to envision serving in a slum in Indonesia for years and years alone. God was giving me a gift I had never allowed myself to hope for—a future husband to serve alongside me in this new community.

Now in April 2012, we watched the building of my new house, which we deliberately made larger than I "needed," as we imagined it becoming a place to teach children in the coming months and years. Homes were not allowed to be fully "permanent," so we constructed the first meter of the vertical walls out of cement blocks, while the upper half was made from woven bamboo. Since the slum had no legal electricity and no water source, we had to pay someone to drill a hole for a water pump and had to pay for a large electrical cable to run electricity to our house.

After a time of fasting and praying, Yosiah decided to quit his salaried job in May 2012 and serve full time in the new slum community. His parents thought he was crazy and could not understand why he would throw away his university education to play in a slum with dirty children. A female Indonesian Bible school graduate was living with me at the time as part of a one-year ministry internship, and so we became a team of three, praying, exploring the slum, and meeting the neighbors together in this new slum community. Lisa, along with a HNGR intern from Wheaton College who had just arrived to intern with our team, remained in inner-city Jakarta. We met at our team center weekly for times of sharing, worship, and prayer.

In January 2013, a few days after my two-year anniversary of moving to Indonesia, Yosiah and I were married in our Mennonite church, and he joined me in living in the slum.[2] We discovered that the bamboo walls were not only see-through but also failed to keep out rain or wind. Over the coming years, our home went through various renovations as, bit by bit, we tried to make it more livable. We eventually covered the bamboo walls with plywood to keep out peeking eyes, rain, and mosquitos.

What started as a coloring and UNO club with neighborhood kids grew into "lessons" twice a day. Morning lessons were for the kindergarten-aged kids, and afternoon lessons were for the elementary children after they got home from their schools. We quickly realized that having seventy kids in our house a day was not sustainable and so decided that it was time to build on the plot of land next to our house. For the front door of the new school,

---

2 Prior to being married, Yosiah lived with his parents and commuted daily back and forth to the slum community.

we brought the door from my old home with Lisa, where I first lived after moving to Jakarta. The tree with the painted handprints of the children had come with us, and House of Hope was opened in April 2013.

We had felt the devastation and grief of watching a slum die, but now we were watching this slum be born and grow up right before our eyes. We saw banana trees get chopped down to make roads, land cleared for new homes, new families moving in all around us. Slum communities are constantly growing and changing. This new slum community started out fairly sparsely populated, with lots of greenery and a more rural feel. Over the years, hundreds (thousands?) of new families have moved to this land and most of the green space has been replaced by homes. Homes are a mix of very basic shacks and more permanent dwellings constructed with cinderblocks.

During the rainy season, muddy roads created obstacle courses that we had to trudge through in order to get anywhere. When Yosiah's motorcycle wheel got completely jammed with the red, sticky mud, he had to get off, remove the wheel, and manually clear out the mud. More than once, our sandals disappeared in knee-deep mud, never to be seen again. Mud-boots became a necessary part of our wardrobe.

Dry season presented different challenges, as the tall meadow grass became brittle and yellow, the perfect fuel for fire. Multiple times, men in the community had to rush out to fight back flames when the grass caught fire. One day, we were teaching kids in our living room when our next-door neighbor came politely to the window. "Kak, can you please turn on your water machine? The fire is very big." Yosiah ran to the window, saw the flames, and ran to turn on our water hose. Meanwhile, I evacuated the students to the open ball field near our house. Thankfully, no houses caught fire. But during the dry season, we still worry about fires. We now keep our passports and other important documents in one place and have an evacuation backpack ready to grab if needed.

After years of moving from one place to another, God had finally planted me in a new home. There are no guarantees in slum settlements, as we are only squatters, borrowing the land until someone with more money claims ownership and kicks us off, but we moved to this community in May 2012, and we are still here today— ten years later! Our team has seen many transitions, with people coming and going. Our family has had many transitions as well—from singleness, to marriage, to parenting two sons.

We have planted our family here, along with a mango tree, and we are watching everything grow with gratitude and amazement. Though I left my previous slum community weeping, I have trusted that *those who sow in tears will reap with songs of joy. She who goes out weeping, carrying seed to sow, will return with songs of joy, carrying sheaves with her (Ps 126:5–6). The Lord has brought me through the valley of tears (Ps 84:6), and my heart is full and singing with joy.*

Chapter 7

Finding Treasures in Trash

*If you will only remain in this land, then I will build you
up and not pull you down; I will plant you, and not pluck
you up; for I am sorry for the disaster that I have brought
upon you. Do not be afraid ... as you have been; do not be
afraid ... says the LORD, for I am with you, to save you
and to rescue you... I will grant you mercy.*
–Jeremiah 42:10–12a

"I need to ask Kak Anita for help," Ibu Yulie, one of my close friends in the new neighborhood, said to me. (In Indonesia, it is more polite to refer to the person you are speaking to in third person.) "But don't be mad," she added pleadingly. I looked at my friend, who was four feet, eight inches tall. Her left eye had been injured as an infant, leaving her blind in that eye. She held her two-month-old baby on her lap, draped in traditional batik fabric.

This strong woman in front of me was raising three young kids on her own while her husband worked a two-year contract job on a Korean tanker ship. He had missed a lot this year: the birth of his third child and the first day of first grade for his oldest daughter.

During our first month in this new slum community, we got to know Ibu Yulie and her family, as their shack was right behind our house. At the time, Ibu Yulie was nine-months pregnant. When she went into labor, she tried to give birth at the local midwife's clinic. But after twenty-four hours, the midwife told Ibu to go to the hospital, and so she had asked Yosiah to take her.

But Ibu had no money to pay for a hospital birth. So Yosiah had rushed around, filling out the legal paperwork so she could get everything free. Thankfully, unlike many of our neighbors, Ibu Yulie had the necessary identity card and local paperwork to be able to access free health care. After *Dede*[1] was born, our Indonesian female teammate spent the night in the hospital to support Ibu, and the next morning, Yosiah and I brought Ibu and Dede home by taxi.

---

1 *Dede* is the term for younger sibling.

Now, Ibu sat before me with two-month-old Dede, her face tight with worry. "Our boss went home to the village for a couple days," she said. Ibu, her three children, and her mother survived by recycling garbage. Her mother went out twice a day, morning and afternoon, to collect anything of value. Her old body had been worn down by years and the harsh burden of poverty. With a full sack of recycling over her shoulders, she always walked slowly and yet looked regal to me in her batik skirt and Muslim head covering. Her wrinkled skin revealed both wisdom and beauty.

"Our boss went home, and now we haven't had anyone to buy our recycling," Ibu continued. "It's a few days late already." In Jakarta, the poorest of the poor look for recycling, then sell it to a Boss, who sells it to a higher-up Boss, who comes in a truck to collect it. With any profit divided between so many people, those who sort through the garbage looking for recycling barely scrape by, earning just enough rupiah to eat each day. Ibu's mother brings in about twenty dollars every two weeks, which is hardly enough for rice and vegetables. They cook over a wood fire now, since it is too expensive to buy oil for their little stove, so Ibu's mother has to gather sticks and scraps of wood to burn.

"Can I borrow two dollars from Kak Anita to buy rice?" Ibu finally asked. "The past three days we've made a few cups of rice last, but now that is gone." In the distance, we could hear her middle child crying.

"Sugi's coming for me," she laughed. Sugi, an adorable two-year-old boy, arrived at my front door in tears as I handed Ibu Yulie the money.

"I'm hungry. I want to eat!" he said. Ibu smiled, thanked me profusely, and headed to the corner store to buy rice.

Living in this community, we constantly have to ask ourselves: What does it mean to be a good neighbor? What does it mean to love our neighbors? To love Jesus by loving them? How do we use money wisely? How do we avoid doing harm?

From the beginning, we set a precedent that we did not want to be viewed as ATMs, and so people rarely ask us for money. In rare instances, as with Ibu Yulie, we give small amounts to help people survive. On other occasions, we have given larger amounts for school fees, medical costs, or births. Yet we do not want money to ruin the relationships we have worked so hard to build, and so we have found that giving is better than loaning, as loans might cause a break in the relationship if people cannot repay them and feel ashamed.

> How do we use money wisely? How do we avoid doing harm?

The majority of the people in our community make their livelihoods through collecting garbage (*tukang sampah*) and scavenging recycling (*pemulung*). The fathers and older sons do the garbage routes, pulling a cart by hand or towing it with their motorcycle. They collect garbage from middle-class neighborhoods, then dump it in our community, which has formed a mini trash mountain.[2] Then women and children sift through the trash, sort out anything that is recyclable, and sell it for extra money. Both tukang sampah and pemulung are almost entirely Sundanese people, who are native to the island of Java and have a rich cultural heritage.[3] Being Sundanese is virtually synonymous with being Muslim. Our neighbors' home villages are only a two-hour motorcycle ride away from Jakarta, and so most of them keep close ties to their relatives back home. Those who have their own motorcycles frequently travel home on weekends or whenever there is a family wedding, circumcision, or health crisis. Over time, we noticed that the Sundanese section of the slum was expanding, as more and more relatives moved from their village to seek a better life in Jakarta.

When we visit churches in the United States and share about our lives in Jakarta, people often ask us why people leave the beauty of a rural village life to come to a mega-city and pick through garbage. Our Sundanese friends have told us, "In the village, trash is trash. In the city, trash is money. The important thing is humbling yourself to do the work—and you will be able to make money." Most of our Sundanese neighbors have homes in the village, but they do not have ways to make money. Their parents often worked as contract rice farmers, who did not own their land but worked as day laborers for rich landowners. Coming to the city to seek a livelihood is appealing, even if it means literally digging through the city's trash.

"When I was sixteen and got married," my friend Mama Sari told me, "we moved here right away. We started from nothing. My husband did not even have his own garbage route, but he went along helping his uncle.

---

2 The mini "trash-mountain" was an illegal dumping site. After a few years, government authorities swept in, posted signs forbidding dumping more garbage and threatening violators with large fines. Now trash-mountain has turned into real-estate, and new shacks are being built every day. Many of our students come from on top of this former dump site.

3 The Sundanese are the second-largest people group in Indonesia, numbering more than forty-five million. The largest people group are the Javanese, who number over a hundred million. According to the Joshua Project, the Sundanese people are the tenth largest unreached people group in the world. Less than 0.49 percent are Christian adherents, and only 0.05 percent are evangelical.

Little by little, we saved and then were able to buy our own garbage route.[4] At first, I did not like it here—the flies, the trash, the rats—it made me want to vomit. But I had no choice. And anyway, now I am used to it," she says with a laugh.

Most of our Sundanese neighbors are first-generation slum dwellers, who came to this neighborhood around the same time that we did. They retain a sense of village life even here—keeping close-knit family and communal ties, celebrating rituals and rites of passage together, and continuing to speak their Sundanese language. Children grow up bilingual, speaking Sundanese in the home and Bahasa Indonesia with non-Sundanese friends and in school.

My friends from the previous inner-city slum community were mostly Javanese, and in this new slum, they created a distinctly Javanese corner of the neighborhood, speaking Javanese amongst themselves and switching to Bahasa Indonesia to interact with non-Javanese friends and neighbors.[5]

For the most part, our Javanese friends had grown up in Jakarta, either being born in the city or moving here as young children. Generally, the Javanese are not pemulung, but work as motorcycle drivers, taxi drivers, food vendors, or singer-beggars. There are many ways to beg in Jakarta. Some of our neighbors used to train monkeys to do tricks, but now that is illegal. Some dress up in big costumes and dance on the side of major roads. Others paint themselves silver and carry cardboard boxes around, singing for donations. These ways of begging are creative and help people retain a sense of dignity—since they are doing something, it is not technically begging. Many Javanese women work as maids in middle-class homes, washing laundry and cooking.

Over the years, we have tried to tread carefully between these two different culture groups. The neighbors on our street are entirely Javanese, but the majority of our students tend to come from the Sundanese pemulung families. We feel humbled and grateful for the amazing opportunity to get to know these beautiful people and to bear witness to the love of Christ amidst two people groups that

---

4 Often to get a job as a garbage collector, one must purchase the job from the man who previously did that route. In 2022, the going rate for one garbage route was around $600, a huge sum for our neighbors. In essence it is similar to purchasing a small business.

5 The Javanese culture and language has a variety of different types. Our neighbors are part of the Javanese Pesisir Lor culture group, which numbers around thirty-seven million, with 2.8 percent adhering to Christianity (and only 0.01 percent evangelical). According to the Joshua Project, this makes them the twelfth largest unreached people group in the world.

rarely have the opportunity to hear about Jesus. We continue to ask ourselves what it means to seek the kingdom of God in this place and how to share *truly good news* about Jesus rather than perpetuating Christianization, Westernization, or colonization.

As I live within this garbage collecting and recycling community, I am learning about God, the pemulung, who sorts through mountains of trash day after day, searching for anything of value. Back in first-century Palestine, Jesus called out to Simon and Andrew, "follow me and I will make you fish for people" (Matt 4:19). Two-thousand years later, I imagine Jesus coming to this place and saying, "Follow me, and I will make you pemulung of people!" Jesus tells those whom the world views as garbage, "You have value. Though others have cast you off, you are a treasure." As we follow Jesus, our pemulung, to the trash heap, he is longing for us to help him build up those who have been pushed down, plant and nourish those who have been uprooted, be merciful to those who have experienced disaster, and encourage those who are afraid (Jer 42:10–11).

> I imagine Jesus coming to this place and saying, "Follow me, and I will make you pemulung of people!"

Sighs Too Deep for Words

We know that the whole creation has been groaning in
labor pains until now; and not only the creation, but we
ourselves, who have the first fruits of the Spirit, groan
inwardly while we wait for adoption, the redemption of
our bodies. For in hope we were saved. Now hope that is
seen is not hope. For who hopes for what is seen? But if we
hope for what we do not see, we wait for it with patience.
Likewise the Spirit helps us in our weakness; for we do
not know how to pray as we ought, but that very Spirit
intercedes with sighs too deep for words.
–Romans 8:22–26

My first few years in Indonesia, I had the same "twenty question" conversation countless times. People would ask, "Are you from Australia?" "Did you know Obama grew up in Indonesia?" "Obama likes *bakso* soup, do you like it?" "Do bules *just* eat cheese and bread?" "Is it true that Americans never eat rice?" While the repetition of these questions sometimes got annoying, I enjoyed the banter and would laugh as I answered their successive questions. The conversation would turn more serious when they inevitably asked, "Why would you leave beautiful, clean America to come live in this crowded, dirty slum?" or "Why don't you live in wealthier neighborhoods like other foreigners?"

Depending on the person, I might say, "I am interested in learning Indonesian culture and language. If I lived in a wealthy gated community, where neighbors rarely talk to each other, I couldn't practice language. Living in this community makes it possible to interact with lots of people." This answer makes sense to people and also affirms the positive elements in their communal way of life and communicates that I value the experience of living near them.

My longer, more vulnerable answer would be, "I am a follower of *Isa Al-Masih* (the qur'anic name for Jesus). When *Isa Al Masih* walked this earth, he often spent time with the poor and vulnerable. I want to follow him and learn from him in this place." Sometimes, this ended the conversation, since people feel more comfortable laughing about eating bread and cheese than discussing religion. But other times, this response became a bridge to talking about Jesus and my desire to follow him. Our team did not hide the fact that we were followers of Jesus, but we wanted to find culturally appropriate ways to share with our Muslim neighbors. One way we found was through prayer.

One day, early in 2013, we were invited to the engagement ceremony of the eldest daughter of close friends. When it was time to take pictures of the newly engaged couple, the next-door neighbor called my husband and me outside and asked for our help because the mom of the engaged girl had lost consciousness.

We found Ibu Asmi laying down on an old couch out back. Her hands clenched ours tightly, and her eyes looked at us in anger and fear, but she could not talk. We began praying and immediately realized that she was not sick, but had a spirit raging within her. For two hours, we prayed for our friend. When we said the name of Jesus, she clenched our hands more tightly, pointed at us, and ground her teeth while thrashing back and forth. Finally, they called an old holy Muslim man to say some prayers and spit holy water on her, but the spirit would not leave.

After two hours, the spirit began to speak, but its voice was not Ibu Asmi's. Ibu was a tiny, skinny, weak woman, but the voice that came from her mouth was a deep man's voice, who said he was the spirit of her father and was angry because he had not been informed about the plans for his granddaughter to get engaged that day. We continued to pray fiercely as the spirit thrashed Ibu around, for she gripped our hands with a power not her own.

After throwing several wild punches, Ibu Asmi finally relaxed, then opened her eyes. Though exhausted, she called to us in her own voice, saying weakly, "*Kak Yosiah? Kak Anita? Berdoa Kak. Berdoa.*" ("Yosiah. Anita. Pray. Pray.") So we prayed more.

When we had finished, she thanked us, and we went home.

The following day, we visited her, and she could not remember anything about the previous evening.

When I first arrived in Indonesia and began hearing stories about spiritual warfare, I was skeptical since praying for demon-possessed people was not part of my church upbringing or college education. But most of our Sundanese and Javanese neighbors—as well as most Indonesian Christians, including my husband—are familiar with spiritual warfare and it seemed evident I needed to learn about it, too.

For our Sundanese and Javanese neighbors, there is no clear separation between the spiritual realm and the physical realm. They use amulets, charms, special prayers, and rituals to ward off evil spirits, especially during rites of passage, such as marriages, pregnancies, births, and other significant events. For example, pregnant women are told to carry around knives, pin garlic on their shirts, and carry a piece of a wicker broom when they go out—especially at night. Parents also pin garlic to the clothes of newborn babies, lay rice next to them in a bottle, and place a knife by their sides to keep the evil spirits at bay.

As Christians, our family believes that Jesus has power over evil spirits and offers freedom and good news for those who are trapped in the bondage of fear. We have experienced these principalities and powers in dreams and in more subtle ways. We realize that our battle is not against flesh and blood. There are forces that do not like what we are doing. But prayer is not only about casting out demons.

We have never had anyone refuse the offer of prayer. By offering to pray for our neighbors, we show love to them and demonstrate that we are people of faith who follow *Isa Al-Masih*. We have prayed for sick friends, people going through financial or marital difficulties, those needing wisdom in decision-making or regarding the schooling of their children. Those who receive prayer often pray for us as well.

One morning I was on my way home when I ran into Mama Ali,[1] whose family we have known for years. When we lived in the previous slum community, my teammate Lisa took wedding photos for Ali's mom and her husband. Now, their son Ali is our student. "Where are you heading this morning?" I asked Mama Ali.

"To the hospital to see our daughter," she told me. Her second child had been born prematurely the month before, and Mama Ali told me with tears in her eyes that her daughter had just tested positive for HIV. Both of Ali's parents were HIV positive and had been on treatment for seven years. They most likely got infected through a needle (her husband had used drugs before they were married) or through Mama Ali's former night work on the streets for some years. "My sin is so great," Mama Ali told me. "But why should my daughter have to suffer for my sins?"

A few days later, baby Depi came home from the hospital weighing just 4.5 pounds (2 kilograms). When our family went to visit her, I was shocked

---

1 In Indonesia, it is common to refer to parents by the names of their children. Often, we never learn the parent's name.

at her tiny size. A toddler cousin bobbed about the house, carrying a doll that was about the same size as Depi. Mama Ali and Bapak Ali graciously received us. Since we are some of the only people they have ever told about their HIV status, they shared their grief over their daughter's diagnosis.

"What will I tell her when she is older? Will she hate me?" her mother asked me over and over again.[2]

Bapak Ali was nearly blind from an infection that occurred a few years ago when he stopped his HIV meds. Now he is back on the meds, but the damage to his eyes is irreversible. "If I didn't have my family to think about, I would kill myself," he said with tears in his eyes. "My sins are so many. I wish I could carry in my body all the effects of my sin—not my child! I wish all the sickness could be put on me. I want to bear it, not her."

With his anguished words echoing in my mind, I could not remain silent. I had to tell them about the One who has done just that: borne all sin *on his body*—my sin, their sin, the world's sin—he has carried it all on his body. I tried to explain in as simple words as possible. I told them about Jesus, how he died on the cross, bearing the entire world's sin on his body, and then rose again so that we could be offered this gift of forgiveness.

After about an hour, Yosiah asked if he could pray for them. They gladly agreed, and we all wept as he prayed. Then I hugged Mama Ali and said, "God loves you. God loves your family."

They thanked us and then prayed for us: "May God bless Kak Yosiah and Kak Anita's family with health and provisions always."

With SpongeBob on the TV, children playing noisily on the street, and a child strumming a little ukulele in the same room, there were many interruptions, but the space was sacred. It is for opportunities such as this that we live here. So many of our neighbors would never set foot inside of a church, but we are following Jesus, who invites us to *go outside the camp* with him to seek all who are waiting for adoption, all who are groaning for redemption, all who are aching with sighs too deep for words (Rom 8:22–26).

---

2 After six months of treatment, the doctors retested baby Depi, and she tested negative for HIV. Thankfully, that means she can now stop the medications. Her parents, of course, were overjoyed by this news.

Chapter 9

No More Tears

We do not want you to be unaware, brothers and sisters, of
the affliction we experienced in Asia; for we were so utterly,
unbearably crushed that we despaired of life itself. Indeed,
we felt that we had received the sentence of death so that
we would rely not on ourselves but on God who raises
the dead. He who rescued us from so deadly a peril will
continue to rescue us; on Him we have set our hope that He
will rescue us again, as you also join in helping us by your
prayers, so that many will give thanks on our behalf for the
blessing granted us through the prayers of many.
–2 Corinthians 1:8–11

There was a light knock on my front door, and I said, "*Masuk*" (come in). My neighbor and best friend in the community, Ibu Gusti, entered, her hands full of plates of food—tempeh, fish, vegetable soup, rice. She set the plates down on the counter and said, "*Makan* (eat), while it is still warm. You have to eat so you can regain strength." "*Terima kasih* (thank you)," I said weakly, and she left—another day of me being too sick to cook, another day of Ibu Gusti loving me back towards health.

Dengue fever had me curled up in bed, aching all over, and yet I was still struggling and frustrated by my need for rest. A week of hospitalization in April 2013 had forced me to rest, but now, weeks after my release from the hospital, my body was still so weak and tired. I wanted to receive Jesus's invitation, *Come, weary ones. I'll give you rest*, but this sickness had forced me to realize that I am not good at rest.

While I was in the hospital, Ibu Gusti visited me—bringing guava, pears, and oranges. As I sat in the hospital bed, with IVs in my arm, she braided my hair. For the past month of my sickness, so many people had showered me with visits, emails, letters, and phone calls, telling me to get well soon and to take care of myself, to *rest*.

Living in a slum community has been excruciating at times, testing the very limits of my spiritual, mental, and physical health. Health issues are also a constant battle for our neighbors. We have seen people whose faces are deformed by leprosy or whose legs are crippled by polio. We have watched men and women coughing up blood from tuberculosis. We have sat at the hospital bed of a student, whose jaws were clenched shut with tetanus, praying that he would not die (thankfully, he didn't). We have carried a girl with typhoid fever to the doctor. Before living here, I only knew these diseases by the names of the vaccinations, but now they parade in front of our eyes—measles, rubella, hepatitis, whooping cough (here it is known as "the 100 day cough"). This list goes on and on. Following Jesus (and having more money than my friends in the slum), does not protect me from getting sick. In my first year in this community, I got rubella (even though I had been fully vaccinated), walking pneumonia, and then—just a few months later—dengue fever.

During my month of recovery from dengue fever, I reflected on the Old Testament story about God meeting the prophet Elijah in the desert, as his prayers seemed to echo my own prayers in that season. Elijah had just experienced one of the most incredible victories of his life: God had answered his prayer and sent fire down from heaven to consume his offering, proving to the prophets of Baal that Yahweh was, indeed, the LORD. After this dramatic victory, Elijah ran into the desert to flee Jezebel and Ahaz's wrath, and then he lay down in the sand, depressed, wanting to die. "It is enough," he cried, "now, O LORD, take away my life" (1 Kgs 19:4).

Then he fell asleep, and an angel came to him and touched him, saying, "Get up and eat" (1 Kgs 19:5). Then:

> He looked, and there at his head was a cake baked on hot stones, and a jar of water. He ate and drank, and lay down again. The angel of the LORD came a second time, touched him, and said, "Get up and eat, *otherwise the journey will be too much for you.*" He got up, and ate and drank; then he went *in the strength of that food* forty days and forty nights to Horeb the mount of God. (1 Kgs 19:68, emphasis added)

Just a week before I got sick with dengue, we had celebrated the "victory" of finishing the construction of the school building, House of Hope. Now, I was too tired to know what to ask for and too weak to stand. I needed God's intervention. I needed heavenly cakes baked on hot stones. I needed to lay back down and rest a second time. I needed to learn to go on in the strength of the Lord rather than my own strength. *Lord, teach me to receive your rest, to recognize that I am not God, that I am not a robot that can keep running and running. In my weakness, teach me how to receive from others so that this journey will not be too much for me.*

Though I recovered from dengue in 2013—just as I had recovered from rubella, typhoid, and a variety of other sicknesses—many people do not recover. All too often, I see yellow flags hanging in the street, symbolizing that someone has just died. Our next-door neighbor died of diabetes at the age of forty-five. Another young neighbor collapsed from a heart attack. A sixteen-year-old died of typhoid of the brain. A month-old baby died from malnutrition. Two of our kindergarten children died—one of an unknown fever, the other drowned in the canal that runs through our community.

I still remember the moment in 2015 when Yosiah stopped his motorcycle in front of me on the street and said, "Ori is dead." Sweet Ori—his right hand crippled from birth, his two sets of teeth jutting awkwardly from his mouth, which gave him a very distinct smile.

Ori, whose name literally means "dawn," and his little brother, Abi, had always arrived early for morning lessons—an hour or more before House of Hope opened at 9:00 a.m. Countless mornings, I had shooed them back to their house, telling them, "I haven't even showered yet! The teachers are not ready! Go home for another hour."

Ori had been coming to House of Hope for over two years. Though he was between eight and ten years old (his parents didn't know his age), he was in the most basic class with the younger kids because of his developmental disability. Because of Ori's physical disability, he slurred his speech, and other kids and even adults teased him ruthlessly. He often tried my patience, as I had to repeat simple lessons over and over again, but he was so innocent and eager to learn. And he and his brother loved our school, as it was a respite of peace and love from their crazy home life. Their mother was addicted to gambling—and so rarely took the time to cook the family a decent meal—and their father was an alcoholic—who only had harsh words for the family. Their older brother was a kleptomaniac and frequently got beaten up by neighbors for stealing things.

> Lord, teach me to receive your rest, to recognize that I am not God, that I am not a robot that can keep running and running.

Ori's parents didn't know how he had died—just that he had a fever, perhaps typhoid, dengue, or hepatitis. He was sick for five days, and they thought he would recover, but then he had seizures and died.

When I think about Ori's death, I wonder, *what if* his family had sought us for help on Wednesday or Thursday morning? *What if* we had visited to see why he had not come to lessons for several days? *What if?*

On the Friday of his death and burial,[1] we visited his family to pay our respects. His body seemed so tiny under the batik fabric that covered him. He had never come to Friday lessons, since his family always went to a mosque to beg from the men who attended Friday prayers.

As I stood over Ori's tiny body, I thought of his favorite song at school: "*Burung pipit yang kecil dikasihi Tuhan. Terlebih diriku dikasihi Tuhan.*" (The small sparrows are loved by the Lord. How much more am I loved by the Lord.)

Though I will miss his smiling face at dawn each morning at Hope House, I know that Ori is no longer suffering. No one will call him ugly names or beat him or tease him anymore. Embraced by the Creator, he can finally rest.

As we continue to wrestle with the inequalities and vulnerability all around us, facing "affliction" and "deadly peril," we sometimes feel "unbearably crushed" and "despair of life itself" (2 Cor 1:8–10). Yet as we labor with our physical bodies, we place our hope in the one who "raises the dead" (2 Cor 1:9). And as we groan with the rest of creation for redemption, we long for the day when God will make his home among people: "He will wipe every tear from their eyes. Death will be no more; mourning and crying and pain will be no more, for the first things have passed away" (Rev 21: 4).

> And as we groan with the rest of creation for redemption, we long for the day when God will make his home among people: "He will wipe every tear from their eyes."

---

1 Culturally, burials happen only a few hours after a death—on the same day, if possible.

Chapter 10

Mothering in the Slums

[When struggling with prayer,]
It is good to remember that we are not alone
on this barren coast. … Set a little child in the midst
of your thoughts. See it when it is ill. It cannot say much
to its mother, but it can look its love, and the mother
understands. The frequent little looks of love passing
between mother and child, the frequent little touches of
love, these are the signs of love. The Maker of mothers is
not less understanding than the mothers He has made.
"O more than mother's heart, I come, a weary child,
to Thee."
–Amy Carmichael[1]

When I first joined Servants, I assumed that I would be serving as a single female forever. I never imagined finding a potential husband who would be interested in serving in a slum. But then God surprised me with Yosiah, and as we envisioned ourselves serving together long term, we decided that we would raise our children in this place we had come to love.

I had seen how difficult it was for other couples with children to join Servants and move into a slum, but I also knew that some Servants families in other cities had survived for ten or more years. In the first year of the Jakarta team, two couples with young children had come and gone, which had left me wondering if Servants families could actually survive in a Jakarta slum.

When I was pregnant with our first son in 2014, a family from New Zealand with two beautiful, blond-haired young daughters joined our team for four years. Alisha and Mike inspired us by living very simply in a tiny shack—one bedroom could barely fit a bunk bed for their girls, and the "living room" doubled as the parents' bedroom during the night. They traveled everywhere by bicycle, and everyone in the neighborhood loved them. We did our best to help them transition, but the constant stares (blond-haired girls stick out), questions, pinching of cheeks, and asking for

---

1 Carmichael, *Edges of His Ways.*

photographs were hard to bear. Eventually, they moved to a larger house and settled on a few more sustainable ways of living, and they began to bless the neighborhood by running a sewing livelihood project with women.

I naively thought that my transition to mothering in the slums would be much easier, since I already knew the language and my husband was Indonesian. So I was not at all prepared for how extremely hard that transition would be. My theory is that parents who are in the midst of the hard years are too exhausted to share their experiences with other young couples; and by the time the darkest parts are over, all that the parents remember is the smiling faces of adorable children in the photographs from those young years. And the parents who *have* the perfect sleeping and eating babies do have energy to share, so their stories get broadcast and told more, while those who are struggling are left to feel like they are the minority.

Motherhood ushered me into a hard, yet beautiful new season, as I could relate to the women in my neighborhood in new ways. I chose to give birth at a midwife's clinic instead of in a hospital, and since my neighbors almost always birth with a midwife, they enjoyed this similarity. When we arrived home from the midwife's clinic, more than fifty neighborhood women poured into our house to see our baby, bearing gifts of soap, laundry detergent, and clothes. I enjoyed discussing diapers, nursing, and baby food with these moms, and they taught me how to tie a traditional batik fabric wrap around me to hold my baby. Though I had a baby carrier from America, I realized that the simple batik wrap was much more convenient.

I loved my new son, and his smile brightened our lives, but the sleepless nights, month after month, with no solution in sight, left me physically and emotionally depleted. We later learned that our son had undiagnosed GERD,[2] so he was nursing constantly to soothe his upset stomach. He was a poster child for breast milk, weighing in at a whopping 28.6 pounds (13 kilos) at six months, and my neighbors could not believe that he had not eaten any food yet. When we tried to start feeding him solids at six months, he threw everything up. It took months to figure out what was going on, and meanwhile, I was sleep-deprived, and my mental health was suffering.

Then, when our first son was only twenty-one months old, our second son was born; I had a toddler who still did not sleep well at night as well as a newborn. Somehow, I still washed cloth diapers by hand, and when I look

---

2 GERD stands for gastroesophageal reflex.

back at the photos of all the diapers on the lines now, I wonder, "*What was I thinking?*" Most nights, I fell asleep with my right arm stretched out to my first son, and my left arm wrapped around my nursing baby, my body in the position of the cross. When I remember the blur of those sleepless nights now, I can see how being a mother has taught me more about dying to myself and picking up my cross than any other experience of my life.

Then our second son began to get horrible heat rash for months on end, which woke him up at night to itch and fuss. On weekends, we escaped to our "team center,"[3] where the air conditioning helped relieve his heat rash a bit, but as soon as we returned to our house in the slum, the heat rash would return with a vengeance. We tried everything—topical medicines, oral medicines, dressing him in lightweight clothing, and keeping him from playing in the sun—but nothing seemed to help. I often cried out to God. *If you want us here, why is it so hard? Why can't our boys sleep through the night like other kids? Why is eating such a struggle? It's taking all my energy just to help my children survive—so why are we living here? What's the point?*

I was struggling with postpartum depression, but now wonder if I was actually depressed or just in a mental fog and physically exhausted from not sleeping properly for two years. I felt as if I were trying to swim in a pool of thick mud as I trudged through each day. *How can I possibly offer hope to my neighbors when I can barely cling to hope myself?* I often wondered.

No one had ever warned me that parenthood would change my relationship with God, that my "prayer life" and "quiet times" would never be the same. I felt guilty that I could not read the Bible—or anything else—without falling asleep. I felt frustrated by my inability to focus when I tried to pray. I felt angry that I could not join our church services because there was no childcare provided for young children. I envied my former self, who'd had hours to pray, read Scripture, journal profusely, and join church services multiple times a week.

When we had our first furlough with our two boys in 2016, family and friends lovingly helped me—and I realized that self-care was no longer a choice to be viewed as a luxury. If I wanted to keep living in the slum, I would have to make time to take care of myself—to go for morning runs, to have time to listen to worship music, to go on dates with my husband.

---

3 A house our team rented in a middle-class neighborhood so that we could take turns having a sabbath from life in the slums.

Thankfully, things started to get easier as I began to realize that there are many different phases of life, and parenting young children is a very intense phase. I had to stop comparing myself with people in different stages of life—and especially with my "before-children self."

I slowly began to see that prayer just looks different for a mother of young children. I prayed as I washed dirty diapers. I prayed as I ran around the middle-class neighborhood on my morning runs. I prayed as I nursed my baby and watched my elder son play with his friends. And I slowly discovered that God was present in the mundane, daily parts of life—and that God still loved me even if I could no longer have a regular "quiet time."

Now, as I write this in 2022, my sons are eight and six, and I watch in awe as they play with their neighbor friends. This is their home. They were born here, learned to walk on the grassy field near our house, and fell and scraped their knees on the bumpy uneven roads here. They are comfortable climbing mounds of trash with me to visit friends and rarely complain about the smells or flies. They speak two languages, look mostly Indonesian, and brighten up each and every day of my life. When we go somewhere else—even to America—they are happy to come back home to this community and to their friends.[4]

Eventually, we installed better ceiling insulation and exhaust vents in our house, so our son no longer gets heat rash. We also bought a washing machine and a car (things I never would have imagined in my earlier, simpler days). Though we are not living as simply as I once imagined, we are still living *here*—and for that, I am grateful.

Though it is extremely difficult for families that serve in a slum community—or many other contexts—to survive, by the grace of God, it is *possible*.

> And I slowly discovered that God was present in the mundane, daily parts of life—and that God still loved me even if I could no longer have a regular "quiet time."

---

4 Of course, there are also days when the kids are bored and would prefer an exciting trip to an American playground or children's museum. There are moments when they cry, "Why do we live here?" And moments when I, too, want to cry along.

Chapter 11

Outside the Christian Bubble

Then the king will say to those at his right hand,
"Come, you that are blessed by my Father,
inherit the kingdom prepared for you from the foundation
of the world; for I was hungry and you gave me food,
I was thirsty and you gave me something to drink,
I was a stranger and you welcomed me, I was naked and
you gave me clothing, I was sick and you took care of me,
I was in prison and you visited me." … Truly I tell you,
just as you did it to one of the least of these who are
members of my family, you did it to me.
–Matthew 25:34–40

Once Yosiah and I had children, I could rarely attend church services, because there was no nursery where moms could drop off their babies or toddlers. I often wondered how Indonesian Christian moms attended church—did they leave their children with a grandma or a nanny? When my husband watched the kids and I sat in the church service, I would often get angry and start to cry because the services seemed so irrelevant to my life. I no longer experienced God in the liturgies, the fancy band playing music, or the dressed-up people sitting in pews.

One night, I had a vivid dream that I was being crucified—and the person holding the hammer, nailing my hands to the wooden beam, was a pastor.

I had never intended to become bitter with the church, for I grew up in the church, and most of my schooling experience was in church-run schools: a seminary preschool, a Mennonite kindergarten program, a private Christian middle school, and a missionary-kid high school. The only years that I did not attend a Christian school were elementary school, and my parents were pastors during that time, so I spent a lot of time at their church. I grew up in an almost exclusively Christian bubble, with Christian friends, a Christian family, and a Christian education.

> I wept that we are often so busy creating "perfect" Sunday services and "special" Christmas programs that we can't even imagine making time to pray for—let alone befriend, love, or share the gospel with—our Muslim neighbors.

When I moved to Indonesia, I was no longer surrounded by Christians, but I still loved the church and wanted to receive spiritual nourishment in a church setting (not just with my fellow teammates). After making connections with other Mennonites, I visited a Mennonite Indonesian church—where I eventually met Yosiah. For a time, I found glimmers of Christian community in our Mennonite church, but as we continued to meet Jesus and learn from him in the alleyways of our slum community, it became more and more challenging for me to sit in a church building on Sunday morning, as it seemed like I was visiting a completely different planet from the one where I lived day after day.

During this time, I was thirsty to find Christian community with other moms, so I occasionally attended a women's small group at our church. One Saturday evening in November 2018, after we sang together, listened to a teaching and announcements, we divided into four groups to pray. I was excited for the chance to share our prayer requests and pray for one another, but then each group was instructed to pray for one of the following four topics: (1) the church service the following day, (2) the women's Christmas service the following Saturday, (3) plans for the Christmas service coming up in December, or (4) the pastor and his family.

After this women's small group meeting, I sat outside and wept for the church and for the broken world. I wept that we have become so inwardly focused that we only know how to pray for ourselves. I wept that we are often so busy creating "perfect" Sunday services and "special" Christmas programs that we can't even imagine making time to *pray* for—let alone befriend, love, or share the gospel with—our Muslim neighbors.

As I reflected on these experiences of feeling that the church services were a completely different planet from my life in the slum, I realized that there are two sets of cultural walls that separate most of the church-goers in Indonesia (or America, for that matter) from those on the other side of those walls. First, to keep our church communities comfortable, we have erected walls between Christianity and Islam, which have drastically different contexts, cultures, and ways of worshipping and talking about God. Second, to keep our church communities safe, we have erected walls between those who are wealthy or middle-class and those who dwell in slums. Trying to build a bridge between one of these divides is very difficult—such as when a middle-class Christian befriends a middle-class Muslim, or when a wealthy Christian moves into a slum in a Christian context. But bridging *both* of these divides sometimes feels impossible—and this is what Yosiah and I are trying to do as we seek to love our Muslim neighbors in the slum.

Frozen by a fear of what is unknown and different, many Christians do not know how to take the first step to bridge a cultural divide—let alone try to break down these barrier walls. Many people have told us that "mission" should mean starting a church (i.e., building church buildings) in another country or at least on another island in Indonesia—not serving the poor here in Jakarta. In our early days of serving in the slum community where we now live, an elder from our Indonesian Mennonite church came to visit us. At first, we were thrilled that someone from the church was interested in our work, but she ended up trying to convince Yosiah that he needed to "get a real job" and only do ministry in his "spare time." Because I was a foreigner, she put me on a missionary pedestal, but as Jesus himself said, it is hard for a prophet to be accepted in his own hometown; many Christians judged Yosiah for his decision to minister full-time in a slum.[1] Some people think we are crazy to live here with our family, but mostly people think this is something that *we* do and that *they* never need to become involved. Once, as I walked around the community with a visiting Christian woman, she told me quite seriously, "I would not live here, even if you literally paid me a million dollars!"

Back when I was in language school, a classmate told me frankly: "People should only interact with those who share their same socio-economic status. What would I have to say to a beggar in a train station? Absolutely nothing." While many people would not be this brutally honest, I think her sentiments actually reflect the mindset and praxis that most of us believe: *only interact with those who are similar to you—do not cross economic or cultural barriers.*

Churches that do try to interact with the poor often only give away free stuff. While giving physical items is not in itself a bad thing, it is not always helpful either. Too often, those who are financially "wealthy" only view poverty as a *material* problem, but if that were true, then giving material

---

1 John records Jesus saying, "A prophet has no honor in the prophet's own country" (John 4:44); Luke records Jesus saying, "No prophet is accepted in the prophet's home town" (Luke 4:24); Matthew records Jesus saying, "Prophets are not without honor except in their own country and in their own house" (Matt 13:57).

items—such as clothes, food, and money—would solve everything. Yet poverty is a much more complex problem, and giving away "free stuff" often leaves the "wealthy" feeling good about themselves for helping "the poor," who are left feeling dependent, disempowered, and sometimes worse off.[2]

We experienced this dynamic ourselves after a church contacted us, asking if they could collect things for our school as a project for their "mission month." Normally, we try to avoid giving away "free stuff," but in this situation, we thought it was important to pursue a relationship with the church. So we agreed, but very specifically told them what would be useful. Months later, they delivered fifteen boxes full of junk. Included in one of the boxes was a large stack of old underwear.[3]

If we give something broken, old, and ugly to the poor, what does it cost us? If we only give away things that have no value, what does this reveal about our hearts? Because we have erected fences and walls to separate ourselves from people who are not like us, we cannot see that Jesus is standing in front of us as "one of the least of these" (Matt 25:40).

We need to open our eyes and see Jesus on the streets, scavenging through trash. We need to see Jesus in the sick and the hungry. We need to see Jesus in those who are homeless and wearing tattered clothes. Rather than giving worthless gifts to those racked by poverty and suffering, let us remember that whatever we give to "the least," we are giving to Christ *himself.*

Jesus does not want or need our old underwear!

Though I am forever grateful for our brothers and sisters around the world, who support us financially, pray for us, and love across the miles so that we can remain here, I still long for a loving faith community in Jakarta that is seeking to care for those who are struggling with poverty. I still long for more workers to join us—not only in our slum, but in other slums in Jakarta and throughout Asia and the world. I long for people to come and *join the work*—rather than just sending money. I long for more Christians to respond to God's call to love "the least of these" and to live as his hands, washing the feet of the poor amidst the slums of the world.

Of course, not everyone is called to the slums, and we each have to "find our own Kolkata."[4] But as followers of Christ, we are all invited to

2 Fikkert and Corbett, *When Helping Hurts.*

3 Rahma, "Jesus Doesn't Want," Servants to Asia's Urban Poor, July 22, 2021.

4 This phrase is credited to Mother Teresa.

look for opportunities to dig through walls and cross divides so that we can find our suffering Savior among "the least"—whether in a psych ward or a soup kitchen, as we befriend immigrants or strike up a conversation with someone who looks very different from us. Of course, not everyone is called to slums, but more than one billion people in our world are living in slums—and very few Christians are intentionally living and ministering there.

I still find it difficult to go to church, especially around Christmas—with all the preparation that starts months in advance, the huge Christmas budgets, the special clothes, all the kids' programs. With so much energy put into our Christmas preparations, we often forget to welcome Christ in the face of the stranger we pass on the street or the beggar we pass on the corner, even as we celebrate his coming to earth.

Amy Carmichael left Ireland to become a missionary in India, where she spent more than sixty years (never returning to Ireland for a furlough), and eventually died among the people she loved. She is most famous for her work rescuing girls and boys from temple prostitution. She was also a prolific writer,[5] and she tells a story about nurturing a tiny, malnourished orphaned baby. She knew that the milk powder she had at the time would not give enough nutrition to this little baby, and so she went to a nearby church. It was Christmas Eve, and the church was full of worshippers. She tried to find anyone who would be willing to nurse this orphaned infant back to health, for the love of God, but no one was willing, and the baby died.

Jesus is outside, beyond our walls, on the other side of our fences, naked and thirsty, hungry and homeless, longing to be held and loved, dying for someone to help.

Jesus, come to us and free us from the prison of ourselves.

> Rather than giving worthless gifts to those racked by poverty and suffering, let us remember that whatever we give to "the least," we are giving to Christ himself.

5 For a profound overview of Amy Carmichael's life, which has deeply inspired me, see Elisabeth Elliot's, *A Chance to Die: The Life and Legacy of Amy Carmichael.*

Chapter 12

The Word That Shall Not Return Empty

For as the rain and the snow come down from heaven,
and do not return there until they have watered the earth,
making it bring forth and sprout,
giving seed to the sower and bread to the eater,
so shall my word be that goes out from my mouth;
it shall not return to me empty,
but it shall accomplish that which I purpose,
and succeed in the thing for which I sent it.
–Isaiah 55:10–11

One morning in 2017, I gathered up my courage and approached a group of mothers as they waited for their children to finish kindergarten lessons. "*Ibu-ibu* [Moms], there are many stories about the prophets. Would you like to study them together?" My heart was racing as I wondered what the response might be.

Years earlier, I had arrived in Indonesia thirsty to learn more about contextual ministry in a Muslim setting, but I didn't know who might be able to teach me—and didn't know who to ask, since some Christians frown on the idea of contextual ministry.[1] During my senior year in college, I had written a research paper on contextual ministry in an Islamic context, which had been inspired by my semester abroad in the Middle East. On our whirlwind travels, we visited Egypt, Jordan, Israel/Palestine, Greece, and Italy, but I still had so much to learn.

During my early months of adjusting to life in Indonesia, as I felt increasingly hungry to learn more about contextual missions, some foreign friends came to visit my host family. While we ate lunch together, we had a quiet conversation in English, and I voiced my desire to learn more about contextual ministry. The foreign visitor told me that I could get contextual holy books in the same city as my language school and said, "If you ask

---

1 There are countless books, articles, and websites about various ways of ministry in Islamic contexts. See Travis, "The C1 to C6 Spectrum," 407–8. See also Woodberry, *From Seed to Fruit.*

the right people, you should find what you are looking for." Though he did not give me answers, this conversation encouraged me to keep searching. After he left, I remember falling on my knees and asking the One who knows all things to connect me with the right resources and people. Later, I asked some friends from language school, and they knew where I could buy the holy books and also connected me with other resources all in Bahasa Indonesian.

The Qur'an teaches that there are four holy books: *Taurat* (Arabic for the Hebrew word, "Torah," which refers to the first five books of Moses, but could also be interpreted as all of the Old Testament), *Zabur* (the Psalms), *Injil* (the New Testament), and the Qur'an. Most Muslims can list the names of the four holy books, but generally have never seen any holy book except the Qur'an. The holy books had Hebrew or Greek in the side columns, showing the native language for that book—just as the Qur'an has Arabic. The books were beautiful, with blue or maroon covers, instead of black like most Christian Bibles. For Muslims, black is the color associated with hell—so it is not an appropriate color for a holy book. When I first moved to Jakarta, my suitcase was ridiculously heavy because I had filled it with Taurats and Injils—praying that one day I would be able to share them with interested neighbors.

Though I could barely speak Bahasa Indonesia those first months, I remember having a limited conversation with my host family regarding *Isa Al-Masih* (Jesus). I asked my host mom and sister what the Qur'an teaches about Isa Al-Masih, and they seemed happy to talk about it and called my host dad in so that he could give a more complete response. "*Nabi Isa* [Nabi means prophet] was sent from God," he told me, "born of the virgin *Miryam* [Mary], had miraculous power to heal the sick, was the *kalimat-Allah* [Word of God], was taken up to heaven to be with God, and on the last day will come back to judge the living and the dead." Then they asked me, "What does the Bible say about Isa Al-Masih?" At the time, I did not have the vocabulary to answer, but I thought, *What an amazing list of beliefs we share regarding Jesus.*

My host family also asked me a lot of questions about Christianity, including: "What are Easter eggs?" "What is the difference between Easter and Ascension?" (Both are holidays on the Indonesian calendar.) "Is it true that Americans have wedding rehearsals? Why?" I did my best to answer, laughing at what seemed like amusing questions. Now, I realize that these questions reveal all the cultural baggage that has enveloped Christianity.

When my friends think of "Christianity," they literally think it means Western culture—Easter eggs, suits and ties, wearing shoes into a church building with a steeple, scantily clad females on stage singing (like they see on TV), and having wedding rehearsals. Obviously, none of these culturally strange things have anything to do with the gospel of Jesus!

All these conversations and the connections that unfolded with contextual resources launched me on the exciting journey that continues to this day. In 2017, I began learning about Discipleship Making Movements (DMMs), which are fast-growing, indigenous movements that use simple methods to multiply groups of disciples.[2] Our team also learned how to access more contextual resources in Bahasa Indonesia and read books that equipped us with simple tools that we could adapt to our context.[3]

While we cannot control God's Spirit to *make* a movement happen, the stories we read about what God was doing around the world through DMMs inspired us and shaped our prayers and dreams for the work unfolding here in Indonesia.

During this season, as I prayed about our dreams for the future, I felt led to start a Scripture study group with some of my Muslim neighbors.[4] My new teammate Alisha, who was a trained nurse, had been teaching our students' moms basic lessons on health topics (such as high blood pressure, cholesterol, exercise, healthy diets, and dental care). But after a few months, Alisha felt led to focus her energy on a women's livelihood sewing project in the neighborhood, and so this seemed like a natural segue for me to talk with these moms about studying Scripture together. Though I knew these women well, my heart was pounding as I said, "*Ibu-ibu* [Moms], there are many stories about the prophets. Would you like to study them together?" Muslims honor twenty-five prophets—and most are Bible characters, including Adam, Noah, Abraham, Lot, Job, Elijah, Elisha, John the Baptist, and Jesus.

I held my breath as I awaited their answer.

"Sure. Yes. Okay. Let's do it," six women agreed.

So on Friday mornings, while their children attended our free school, these moms gathered in my house to study the prophets together. Over the

---

2 For more information about DMMs, see www.dmmfrontiermissions.com.

3 Two books were particularly helpful: Jerry Trousdale, *Miraculous Movements*, and James Nyman, *Stubborn Perseverance*. *Stubborn Perseverance* (which came to me in Bahasa Indonesia) tells the story of one movement taking place in Indonesia.

4 In DMM circles, these groups are referred to as "Discipleship Bible Studies" (or DBS).

next several months, we worked our way through fourteen stories from the Old Testament, eventually making our way to Jesus.

Each week, we started by answering two simple questions: "What are you thankful for this week?" and "What has been hard this week?" Most of my neighbors had never been asked these questions before, and as the women genuinely shared what was happening in their lives, we came to know each other in profound ways.

After this time of sharing, we reviewed the previous week's story, and then I would read a new passage once, and then one of the moms would read it a second time. Then I invited the women to "story it back to the group" in their own words. As the women repeated the story in their own words, we worked together to remember the details. Then we each responded to three simple questions: *What do we learn in this story about God? How does this story impact my life? Who will I share this story with this week?*

Having grown up in the church, I had heard these Bible stories over and over again in Sunday school, but reading them with friends who had never heard them before helped me hear everything afresh. Ironically, the culture and context of the Bible seemed a lot closer to my Muslim friends' culture than my Western twenty-first century upbringing. My prayer was to be a facilitator rather than a teacher and to trust the Holy Spirit to move and work through Scripture.

After six months, two of the women got jobs as helpers in middle-class homes, one moved away, and the remaining women felt that a group of three would be too small. There is comfort in community—a safety in numbers when discussing new topics. They felt like three was too small a group to continue, so we stopped meeting.

The following year, in 2018, I started another group with five moms, which also lasted about six months. As we journeyed through Scripture together, we moved through the Old Testament stories to the first four stories about Jesus: his birth, his healing power, his walking on water and calming the storm, and his power to cast out demons. Then it was Christmas break, and our family was out of the community for a month.

When we returned to the slum, the women came over for a pizza-making party. I was shocked when one of the women, the spokesperson for the group, told me that they no longer wanted to continue studying the stories. "It would be such a shame to stop," I said as I cut the pizza. All night, I prayed that the other women would show up the next day at our normal time, but no one came.

I was heartbroken—the death of this dream felt like a miscarriage. I had been working so hard for so many years, but it felt like there was little fruit. Though we were teaching children how to read and helping to save people from tuberculosis, and though we were praying for people and having good conversations, I felt like a failure. *Where was the fruit of people meeting Jesus? Would I ever get to see that?* A few months later, we left for another furlough, and these questions haunted me as I shared in churches. *I'm having Bible studies with women in my slum neighborhood*, I would say, and then I would think, *but I have not actually seen anyone come to meet Jesus.* With these words sticking in the back of my throat, I would pray, *Jesus, help me trust that the Word going out from your mouth, will not return to you empty, but will accomplish your purpose and succeed in the thing for which you have sent it.*

Throughout this season, the Lord gently reminded me that I am not in control, for he is God and I am not. I knew that I needed to trust that the months and years of seed planting were not worthless. I needed to hope in God's promise to Isaiah: that God's Word will never return empty. Someday there would be growth—whether or not I would ever see it.

About a year after the women's Scripture study group disbanded, the Lord surprised us by bringing a seeker to our front doorstep. Yosiah was sitting outside on our small porch when he noticed a man he did not know sitting across the street. Yosiah invited the man to come over, and they ended up talking for about an hour, their polite banter eventually turning into a serious conversation. The stranger, Pak Sunoto, was not from our neighborhood, but he liked to walk on the grassy ballfield in front of our house. He had been watching us for years, wondering about the free school we ran in the community, and he had investigated by asking neighbors about us. *Could it really be a free kindergarten? Surely, after a few months, they demand payment?* Our neighbors had told him that we'd been here for years and never charged any fees for the lessons. As Pak Sunoto talked with Yosiah, he had many questions. "You shine," he said. "You have a light—like angels in this community. Why?"

Seeing Pak Sunoto's genuine interest, Yosiah said, "We are followers of Isa Al-Masih. He is why we are here. He is why we do what we do. We believe God has rescued us and greatly loves us, and so we want to share his love with others."

> I knew that I needed to trust that the months and years of seed planting were not worthless.

In the course of this conversation, Yosiah invited Pak Sunoto to come back once a week and study Scripture together—and Pak Sunoto agreed. Journeying for months with this seeker, who was so hungry and thirsty, has been a beautiful experience for us. So we keep sowing seeds, trusting God's Holy Spirit to water them, make them sprout, and bring forth growth. Although there are many reasons to despair, we continue on, very grateful for the surprises—like Pak Sunoto—that the Lord graciously brings to our front door.

Chapter 13

Things as They Aren't[1]

Lord Christ, gentle and humble of heart, we hear your timid call: "You, follow me." You give us this vocation so that together we may live a parable of communion and having taken the risk of an entire lifetime, we may be ferments of reconciliation in that irreplaceable communion called the Church. Show us how to respond courageously, without getting trapped in the quicksand of our hesitations. Come, so that we may be sustained by the breath of Your Spirit, the one thing that matters, without which nothing propels us to keep on moving forward. You ask all who know how to love and suffer with you to leave themselves behind and follow you.
–Brother Roger of Taize[2]

After becoming a mother myself, I discovered how much I love working with pregnant mothers. When my teammate, Alisha, and I were both pregnant at the same time in 2015, we decided to start a "Birth Circle," a term I borrowed from my home church community in the US, which has a monthly Birth Circle, where moms come together to share stories and ask questions about pregnancy, birth, and mothering.

We started meeting once a week, beginning with some basic health topics related to pregnancy and birth and ending with simple exercises. Then we closed our circle by sharing snacks and drinking milk together. On these special afternoons, we gradually got to know one another better, and it was a beautiful gift to journey with these women during this important time in their lives. As the years have gone by, I have shared Birth Circles with hundreds of women, and some of our former elementary students have now become mothers—and now some of their babies are already our kindergarten students!

Year after year, as I have met with an unending parade of pregnant girls and women, I have experienced both joy and sorrow as I have

---

1 This chapter title is a spoof, referring to *Things as They Are* by Amy Carmichael (republished by Good Press in 2019; originally published in 1906).

2 Brother Roger of Taize, *Parable of Community*, 46.

journeyed with my new friends. The injustices in the system continue to be maddening. The cycle of underage marriages and pregnancies is still heartbreaking. *Does this little gathering every week make any difference in their birthing experiences?* I often ask myself.

I remember meeting Dila, who was in one of my first prenatal groups. My first memory of Dila is from a birthday party for a teammate's three-year-old daughter. All the neighborhood kids showed up for the party, even though only twenty or so had been invited. One of the party games was a water balloon toss, where everyone tried to toss the balloon into a hole in a cardboard box. But suddenly everyone started throwing their water balloons at Dila, who was nine at the time. Her mother demanded shampoo from our teammate afterwards!

A few years later, Dila, now twelve years old, was in my prenatal group. She had discovered her pregnancy after having intense pain and going to the hospital, where an ultrasound revealed appendicitis—along with a five-month-old fetus. Her family paid a holy man to perform a religious wedding ceremony with the suspected father, a formality that did not mean Dila and "husband" intended to make a life together. Dila is tiny, even for our neighborhood, and when she was nine months pregnant, she only weighed eighty-one pounds (thirty-seven kilos).

Throughout Dila's pregnancy, she went for regular checkups with the midwife near our slum, but when she went into labor, the midwife turned her down, saying it was too dangerous to have a vaginal birth so recently after having appendicitis. Since Dila's government ID card was from her family's village, they had to transport her, in active labor, to their home village three hours away. She had an emergency C-section, and her baby boy was born healthy.

Miko, her son, was given to Dila's older sister, who was married and still childless after several years. Miko is now one of our students, and he is two weeks younger than our second son. To prevent Dila from having more children out of wedlock, the doctors at the hospital had her (illiterate) father sign papers agreeing to have Dila sterilized. When I think of Dila's story, I pray, *Lord, have mercy.*

I also remember Mama Risa, who always seemed depressed to me—perhaps because she had to raise four young children in a rental room smaller than a one-car garage. Because I was in the process of getting my DONA birth doula certification, I told everyone in the Birth Circle that I would happily attend their births. Mama Risa was the first to take me up on the offer. Her oldest daughter, eleven-year-old Risa, came to get me at two in the morning and told me her mom was in labor. I changed out of my *daster* (house dress), grabbed a granola bar, and we picked our way through the muddy field in the dark to her house. When we got there, the family was already packed and heading out the door to go to the midwife's clinic, so I walked with Risa as her mom rode in a bike cart.

The traditional birth attendant from our neighborhood had already been with Mama Risa for hours, but Mama Risa was very pale, so the midwife hooked up an IV right away, giving her inducing medicines to "help the contractions get better." The midwife was very cold and formal, not at all friendly to Mama Risa. When it came time to push, two other midwives bustled into the room. One midwife pushed on Mama Risa's belly, one yelled at Mama Risa to push, and one pulled the baby's head. I held Mama Risa's hand and tried to encourage her. When a baby girl was born, a midwife took her immediately to a table and swaddled her. No one introduced Mama Risa to her baby or said "good job!" or "congratulations, you have a girl!" So I told Mama Risa about her daughter and kept trying to encourage her.

After delivering the placenta, Mama Risa started hemorrhaging, and I was astonished as I watched her blood fill a large bowl. The midwives worked quickly, injecting medicine and inserting a capsule into her womb, but they criticized Mama Risa, saying, "You didn't take your prenatal vitamins!" and "This is what happens when you have too many kids!" and "If this doesn't stop, we will have to send you to the hospital." Eventually, the blood flow slowed, and I brought the baby girl to Mama Risa so she could breastfeed. But Mama Risa was too tired and asked me to put the baby in the mosquito-net crib. I held the baby briefly, quietly grieving over such a violent birth. I wondered what would become of this baby, what her life would hold.

After taking a picture of Risa and her four siblings, I said goodbye and went home to my family. A few hours later, I came back to visit, and Mama Risa asked to borrow money to pay the midwife. I apologized but said I could not pay, so her family borrowed the money from someone else to pay the $130 in midwife fees. When I remember Mama Risa, I pray, *Lord, have mercy.*

I also remember Puji, a married sixteen-year-old, who joined the Birth Circle early in her pregnancy. She remembered me, as she was married to Dila's older brother (Dila was also in my prenatal group, and I tell her story above). Puji told me she had dated Dila's brother for one month, and then their parents had wanted them to get married. "They were worried we would get pregnant," she told me.

Puji came to every meeting, never missing a day. I praised her for her dedication, but she told me that her father-in-law had said she must attend; this fact intrigued me.

But I was worried about Puji's pregnancy. She had put on a lot of weight during her pregnancy, and I wondered if she might have gestational diabetes. I was also concerned because she hadn't settled on a midwife. I offered to accompany her to the government health clinic to ask for a sugar test and check her hemoglobin levels and was privileged to see her first and only ultrasound.

Then one December evening, there was a knock on our door. Yosiah answered it and was surprised to find Puji's husband and father-in-law at the door. "Puji is in labor," they told him.

"It is *Kak* Anita's responsibility. Where will *Kak* Anita take Puji?"

Yosiah was caught off guard by this statement. "No," he answered, "it is not *Kak* Anita's responsibility. Sorry, she cannot take Puji. Our son is very sick right now."

I came to the door to explain that they could try taking Puji to the nearest midwife, but as far as I knew, Puji had never gotten a check-up there, so the midwife may or may not accept her.

As they walked away, clearly very stressed, I felt awful, but now I understood why Puji's father-in-law had made her come every week—he had thought I would take financial responsibility for the birth! No one else had ever had this misunderstanding, but I was very worried about Puji. What would her labor and birthing be like with no relationship with a midwife and no one that she really trusted to support her in labor?

I found out in the morning that she'd had a C-section. The midwife had agreed to work with her at first, but Puji was already scared, which made her blood pressure rise. The midwife did not want to deal with her and accompanied her to the hospital. The midwife rode a motorcycle, and Puji sat in a cart behind a motorcycle, which was usually used for hauling garbage. I can see it in my head—very pregnant Puji traveling five miles to the hospital in the middle of the night in a garbage cart.

I grieved that this was another C-section that probably could have been avoided. With better prenatal and midwifery care and a labor team that would actually provide support, Puji could have had a positive birthing experience. Whenever I picture Puji, I pray, *Lord, have mercy.*

"*Kak,* we need your help." We have heard these words so many times in our ten years of living in this slum community. Sometimes, this plea is followed by requests for money. Sometimes there are health emergencies, and sometimes homework questions. Each request comes from a person we are trying to love—someone who is a precious human being, not a project or charity case. Each request tugs at our hearts, and we have to discern how to respond with tact and wisdom. This process has taken us a lot of time, and we are often still flooded with guilt when we have to say "no," or struggle with feelings of resentment when we realize that we have been manipulated and a "yes" may have been misguided.

From the beginning of our time here, we have not wanted to be seen as ATMs by our neighbors. We do not want to do harm by throwing money at people's problems. We do not want to create unhealthy dependencies or encourage patterns of free handouts. But we also know that we are extremely rich compared to our neighbors in this community, so we do not want to be stingy either. This is a difficult line to tread, especially when pregnant mothers and the lives of unborn babies are involved.

"*Kak,* I need your help." This day, the woman asking for help is nine months pregnant. Her feet are swollen and her eyes are teary. We have known Mama Sultan for as long as we have lived here. Her son, Sultan, has been part of our school for the past four years. Sultan's two older siblings were some of our first students a decade ago. We have watched their family with grief over the years, as both the older children dropped out of elementary school. Years came and went, but Sultan himself never enrolled in elementary school. Finally, we intervened and helped Sultan apply to a free elementary school for the children of garbage scavengers. Sultan's family are not garbage scavengers, but they barely have any money—so Sultan was accepted.

Sultan's dad has wild, long hair and is a man of prestige in our community, which is fascinating, because he probably did not graduate from elementary school, goes without a shirt most of the time, and sleeps outdoors. However, Sultan's dad knows all the latest gossip about the community, occasionally coaches the neighborhood soccer team, and is involved in all sorts of local slum politics. Yet he does not have a "real" job, and so his family must survive by singing on the streets ("singer beggars" are more respectable than street beggars).

Now, Mama Sultan sits before me and repeats, "*Kak,* we need your help." She is worried about her baby, as the baby's movements have grown more infrequent over the past week. I tell her she should go to a midwife immediately, as there is no way for me to help her. In the past, we have helped with the legal process of making "poor cards" so that our friends can access free government health care in an emergency. Mama Sultan's family, however, does not have any of the legal documents needed to make the card. All their documents were burned in a devastating fire in their previous slum community some twelve years ago. Now, they have no ID card, no marriage certificate, no birth certificates for their older children, and no government family card. Without these documents, our hands are tied. We cannot help.

I want to scream: *Why has it been over a decade and you have not made new paperwork? Pregnancies should not be emergencies—it has been nine months to get to this point. You have had nine months to try to get your paperwork in order for this baby. If you need a C-section, it would be free if you had your papers in order. As it is now, who will pay if you have an emergency and need an operation?*

But I do not scream. I numbly say, "I'm sorry, we cannot help. You need to go to a midwife's clinic." Then I excuse myself to start our Friday morning children's lessons. The interaction replays through my head for days. Should I have given her money? Should I have dropped everything, left our kindergarten students, and accompanied her to the midwife's clinic? I am not sure. As I recall Mama Sultan saying, "*Kak*, we need your help," I pray, *Lord, have mercy.*

> I long for midwives who will see my neighbors as beautiful, strong women—rather than financial burdens to be avoided.

We have prayed for a midwife for this community for many years. We dream of the day when we can open a midwifery clinic, where women can pay-what-they-will for prenatal checkups and delivery. I dream of the day when my precious neighbors will not have to choose between going to a midwife and feeding their family for the day, where checkups are not postponed or avoided because they cannot pay. I long for midwives who will *see* my neighbors as beautiful, strong women—rather than financial burdens to be avoided. I long for midwives who will encourage mothers to breastfeed instead of giving out formula. I long for the day when I can answer Mama Sultan—and the countless others who will come after her—"Yes, we *can* help you."

But we will always be limited. Our efforts will always seem like a drop in an ocean of vast need. We will always feel that we are coming up short—that there is more we *could* have or *should* have done.

But I also believe in a God who is unlimited, a God of abundance. Choosing to live in this place of literal scarcity can lead me into a spiritual battle for hope. *Can I continue to hope and pray for things to be different here? Can I continue to trust that God is good, even when there is so much brokenness around me? Can I believe that God can use my tear-drop efforts to make some sort of a difference in the vast ocean of suffering and desperate need? Can I continue to hope and dream for more followers of Christ to join in this work?*

I pray that my answer to all these questions will be a resounding, "*Inshallah*, if the Lord wills, *Yes*."

> But I also believe in a God who is unlimited, a God of abundance.

Chapter 14

Where Floods and Vermin Do Not Destroy

*Then He answered very quietly, "Much-Afraid, do you love
Me enough to accept the postponement and the apparent
contradiction of the promise, and to go down there with
Me into the desert?" She was still crouching at His feet,
sobbing as if her heart would break, but now she looked
up through her tears, caught His hand in hers, and said,
trembling, "I do love You, You know that I love You.
Oh, forgive me because I can't help my tears. I will go down
with You into the wilderness, right away from the promise,
if You really wish it. Even if You cannot tell me why it has
to be, I will go with You, for You know I do love You,
and You have the right to choose for me anything
that You please."
–Hannah Hurnard[1]*

"We have to wake up the kids now," I said to Yosiah. It was the wee hours of the morning in February 2020, but we had been awakened by the voices of neighbors outside. The street was flooding and already there was water leaking in through the uneven tiles in our bedroom. We started moving our mattresses, hoping the rain would stop, hoping our boys could keep sleeping. But the rain did not stop, and so we woke the boys and sat them on our little table as we scrambled around the house, trying to move things higher. My eldest son had lost his first tooth the night before. In the confusion of trying to lift pillows and mattresses to safety, the tooth got lost in the rising brown flood water.

This was not the first flood to hit Jakarta—only two months earlier, the community had flooded while we were in the United States. During our last week of that furlough, New Year's Eve entering 2020, we received news that a flood had hit our neighborhood. Instead of spending the evening enjoying time with my family, we spent it on the phone with family and friends back in Jakarta. As I imagined what was destroyed in

---

1 Hurnard, *Hinds Feet on High Places.*

our house, I felt numb, with little emotional attachment to anything—until I remembered my guitar. Thinking about that guitar potentially floating in water brought me to tears.

I was used to the transition from furlough back into our slum being hard, as anytime we returned to the US, every home, building, and playground seemed vastly *bigger* than my memories of living there. Then, after six months of furlough, we would get used to everything being larger, and when we returned to the slum, everything would shrink again. This experience is distinctly different from the typical sensation of returning to a place we have not visited since childhood, and it seems so much *smaller* than our memory. But our normal challenges of returning from furlough were compounded and intensified by the recent flood. Our home just seemed so "slummy." I kept thinking, *How can we* possibly *keep living here?*

During those tender weeks, as we cleaned up the January flood damage and tried to find our way back into the regular rhythms of our life in the slum, with all the joys of our friendships as well as the challenges of daily life here, I kept thinking about Jesus's challenging instructions in the Sermon on the Mount:

> So do not worry, saying, "What shall we eat?" or "What shall we drink?" or "What shall we wear?" For it is the Gentiles who strive for all these things, and indeed your heavenly Father knows that you need all these things. *But strive first for the kingdom of God and his righteousness, and all these things will be given to you as well.* So do not worry about tomorrow, *for tomorrow will bring worries of its own.* Today's trouble is enough for today. (Matt 6:31–34, emphasis added)

We were grateful for the prayers, support, and financial gifts that we received from both local and overseas friends during this difficult time, which enabled us to replace everything we needed after the flood.

But those first months of 2020 were dreadfully hard. We all got sick with typhoid, our boys were hospitalized for a week, and now yet another flood. We trudged out of the community, through knee-deep water and prayed that the rain would stop.

Although typhoon rains and periodic flooding make life in the slum more difficult, they also provide hours of fun for the neighborhood children, as the field near our house turns into a gigantic swimming pool. Discarded refrigerators turn into little boats (a fridge is insulated with Styrofoam, so it floats very well), and I sometimes see air mattress or inflatable pool toys drift across the field. The children in our slum have mud wars rather than snowball fights and "flood days" rather than "snow days."

One afternoon, a few days after the second flood, I took the children to play in the field in front of our house, where the water was still knee-deep. From the middle of the field, I saw a covered truck pull up to the nearby road and figured someone was moving in, bringing a truckload of furniture. So I was extremely surprised when a group of youth piled out of the back of the truck, bearing purple balloons and small boxes. I watched them wade through the water and then hand a balloon and what turned out to be a small box of rice to each kid who was playing on the field. "Are you from a church?" I asked. They named a church that I was not familiar with, and then they got in their truck and drove away. "Today I witnessed my first drive-by missions," I told Yosiah sadly.

The ongoing flooding in our slum reminds me that physical possessions are temporary gifts, which I can use to bless others, but I need to hold them with open hands, as another flood could hit at any time. Yosiah and I are still trying to experiment with how we can live out Jesus's teachings regarding possessions in the Sermon on the Mount:

> Do not store up for yourselves treasures on earth, where moths and vermin destroy, and where thieves break in and steal. But store up for yourselves treasures in heaven, where moths and vermin do not destroy, and where thieves do not break in and steal. For where your treasure is, there your heart will be also. (Matt 6:19–21 NIV)

I am fascinated that the NIV uses the word "vermin" here. Other translations say, "rust," but in our slum context, "vermin" makes a lot more sense. We are very familiar with "vermin" (rats) coming into our house and destroying all sorts of things. We often joke that anytime we leave our house for a night, we will come home to find something that has been eaten by rats: the legs of the wooden table that holds our stove, holes gnawed into our bamboo walls, bars of soap in the bathroom, the electrical wires on our washing machine. I may discover bookcases eaten by termites or books rotting with mold (even in our middle-class Sabbath house). Or I might be evicted and have to watch my house get demolished—or burned down.

Rather than hoarding things that will inevitably rot and decay, Jesus invites me to follow him—and to store up different kinds of treasures.

> Physical possessions are temporary gifts, which I can use to bless others, but I need to hold them with open hands

Chapter 15

The Cross and the ER

The community of strangers find their comfort in the cross,
they are comforted by being cast upon the place
where the Comforter of Israel awaits them.
Thus do they find their true home with their crucified Lord,
both here and in eternity.
–Dietrich Bonhoeffer[1]

After a week of diarrhea and vomiting, my four-year-old son was exhausted, but he still had the energy to cry and scream as multiple nurses tried to put an IV in his arm. Finally, after five excruciating attempts, they succeeded, and I breathed a sigh of relief, knowing he desperately needed the fluids. It was Good Friday 2020, during the early months of the pandemic, and we had brought our son to the emergency room because we were worried that he was sick with COVID-19.

> I knew that I could cling to Jesus for comfort because he had suffered on the cross, bearing our griefs and burdens.

As I sat in the ER with my son from nine in the morning until past seven that night, I watched family after family come in, each with their own crisis. Because it was Good Friday, I found myself thinking about Jesus hanging on the cross, and I had a strong sense that Jesus was with my son in his suffering—and with everyone suffering in that ER that day and with the entire world amidst the immense suffering, mourning, and trauma of the global pandemic. I knew that I could cling to Jesus for comfort because he had suffered on the cross, bearing our griefs and burdens. He would not abandon us because he was not locked away in a safe, gated community, but could see us and hear us, and so he would always be with us—even in that emergency room.

I remembered the image I had seen while I was praying after the fire in 2011: the cross perched on top of trash mountain, with Jesus's blood flowing down the side, cleansing the icky brown sewage water into waters of healing. Day after day as I have continued to live in the slums, I have

---

1 Bonhoeffer, *Cost of Discipleship*, 109.

clung to this promise: that Jesus remains present with us, even amidst disgusting, awful, and painful realities.

Everyone knows that the world is filled with both beauty and brokenness—and the world's slums, inhabited by over one billion people, show humanity's best and worst, up close and personal.

When I walk the muddy alleyways of our slum, corrugated metal juts out, threatening to cut me or my children. As we pass haphazardly built shacks, I imagine them toppling in the next big windstorm, their roofs flying dangerously down the alley. In the distance, we can see heaps of trash in various dump sites, a colorful testament to the high price of consumerism. Whenever the trash is burned, the black smoke billows into the grey sky— and into the windows of nearby homes. One season, the trash was dumped and burned only a few yards from our home, and when the wind blew towards us, we had to run around the house, closing windows to keep the black, poisonous smoke out of our house.

We often see children squatting to relieve themselves over the canal that runs through the community and other children swimming in a small pond that is full of raw sewage. It is no wonder that typhoid is so common here or that many people suffer from skin rashes and festering wounds—as well as rat bites. When I visit homes in my neighborhood, my heart often breaks at the ugly, agonizing realities of poverty. As I parent my children in this place, I often struggle with feeling helpless and unsure about how to respond to the overwhelming needs around me.

But living with the urban poor in a Jakarta slum for the past decade, I have slowly realized that I have let go of the illusion that I can make a safe, stable, and independent life for myself and my family. The pandemic has forced the entire world to realize that we are not "gods" who are in control, but rather vulnerable human beings whose lives are interconnected with people all around the world. My neighbors know they do not have enough money in the bank for a health crisis (in fact, most of them do not even have a bank account). They know that sickness, fires, floods, or evictions could come at any time and disrupt their daily life. No matter where we live, we will all have to face suffering, sickness, pain, and grief.

And yet, I have also come to learn that when we find ourselves in a tiny boat in the midst of a storm, with winds and waves crashing around us, we can scream, *Why, Lord? Won't you wake up?*

We can trust God with our fear and anger, because Jesus is in the boat with us. We are not alone.

Won't you speak your words of peace? We can trust God with our fear and anger, because Jesus is in the boat with us. We are not alone. Though so much is uncertain about the future, though people we know and love are sick or dying, though statistics are frightening, though the news is full of depressing stories—we can trust that Jesus is with us in the boat. And as we trust his presence, he will calm our fears and still the raging storm.

Thankfully, the story of Jesus did not stop on Good Friday. The good news is not only that Jesus knows our sufferings, but also that he rose again. As we follow him, we must live as people of resurrection, clinging to the hope that God empowers his people to bring life into places of death.

While I was in the ER with my son that Easter weekend, I read the profound book *Suffering and the Heart of God*, and the following words encouraged me with their precious truth:

> My prayer for you is that you will know him deeply and well, infused with the power of his resurrection, and will willingly enter into the fellowship of his sufferings. When the darkness, the suffering, and the trauma overwhelm you, as they will, get down on your knees and cry out for more of him so that you may persevere until that day when the kingdoms of this world are become the kingdom of our Lord and Christ—that day when the resurrection will mean the redemption of all tragedies, of all things; that day when all suffering will be caught up into the glory of God.[2]

I spent that Easter weekend in the hospital with my son, who received strong IV antibiotics for four days to treat what doctors recorded as a "viral infection" on his discharge papers.

A few weeks after my son was released from the hospital, we were playing in the field near our house, which was littered with trash as usual. As I looked at all the trash, I felt a familiar wave of irritation. Why do people seem to think that whatever they throw on grass will just disappear by itself? For years, I have just ignored the trash, but as I looked out over the field that afternoon, it dawned on me that while my boys were playing with spoons in the dirt or riding their bikes, I could start picking up trash. Several kids joined me at first, and then more observers joined in. We had fun cleaning up together.

Through this living metaphor, God has shown me that even though the world is a mess, I can make a little section of grass look more beautiful. I cannot fix everything, but if I start doing something small and beautiful,

---

2 Langberg, *Suffering and the Heart of God*, 79–80.

others may soon join me—just like the little kids helping me pick up trash. God doesn't ask us to save the world—Jesus has already done that! But God does invite us to serve faithfully, using the gifts he has already given to us. God invites us to share his love and message of hope by loving the people around us—and this includes my own children.

I will never forget the feelings of helplessness and grief that surrounded me that Easter weekend I spent in the hospital with my suffering son, but I will also always remember the tangible presence of Christ—Immanuel, God with us—in the dark valley of that emergency room.

I wrote these words in my journal and set them to music:

> *Jesus, be the air I breathe*
> *The smoke envelops, and threatens to engulf me.*
> *Jesus, be the light I need.*
> *I can't see the way to walk in this darkness.*
>
>> *I find myself in this boat again,*
>> *The wind and waves surround me.*
>> *I know You're Lord of Heaven and earth.*
>> *Won't you speak Your words of peace?*
>
> *Jesus, be the hope I need.*
> *Despair surrounds me, and threatens to drown me.*
> *Jesus, be the Truth I need.*
> *Dispel the lies, replace them with Your Spirit.*
>
>> *I find myself in this boat again,*
>> *The wind and waves surround me.*
>> *I know You're Lord of Heaven and earth.*
>> *Won't you speak Your words of peace?*
>
> *"The LORD, Your God, is with you.*
> *He is mighty to save.*
> *He will take great joy in you.*
> *He will quiet you with his love.*
> *He will rejoice over you with singing."*[3] *Alleluia.*
>
>> *I find myself in this boat again,*
>> *Awake, arise, and save me.*
>> *I know You're Lord of Heaven and earth.*
>> *Thank You for Your words of peace.*
>> *You are the Word of Peace.*

---

3 An adaption of Zechariah 3:17.

A Time to Tear Down and a Time to Build Up

For everything there is a season, and a time for every matter under heaven.
–Ecclesiastes 3:1

That Easter weekend of 2020, as I stayed with my sick son in the hospital, men were literally knocking down our house with sledgehammers. I watched a video of Yosiah walking around the rubble of our home as I lay in the hospital bed with our son and wept. I knew this was not the same as when the Miracle House had been demolished back in 2012; this time we were intentionally renovating our house to make it more sustainable. And I prayed that the tearing down and rebuilding of our home would lead to something better.

I remembered back to our first year in the new slum community in 2012; what started as a coloring group and homework club in our little house had grown into a kindergarten program and elementary afterschool program for about seventy kids a day. Then in 2013 we built House of Hope, a fifty-square-meter building in the lot next to our house, and soon were bursting at the seams of our one room schoolhouse. Eventually, we had divided the single room into three spaces using homemade plywood dividers, but this provided no sound barrier, and so we had to use the "living room" in our house as well as our teammates' small house for overflow classrooms. Just as we were praying about how we might expand our space again, the coronavirus pandemic began, and our team was thrust into a very bare time.

Our bule teammates Alisha and Mike had left in November 2017, and since then we had been a team of all Indonesians (except for me). Then in April 2020, a long-term teammate became extremely ill and had to leave the community indefinitely, and another teammate and her husband stepped down because they no longer wanted to take the risk of being exposed to COVID-19. That left Yosiah, myself, and one teammate to teach seventy kids a day, and so—for the first time since opening—we made the hard decision to close House of Hope for four months as we waited to see what would happen with COVID-19.

Though these months of waiting were very difficult, we prayed in faith and trusted that God would provide for us and for our neighbors. While there has never been a multitude of Christians wanting to move into a slum, the right person has always joined us at the right time, each with a different story, a different journey that brought them here for a time and then eventually took them away.[1] We have mourned having to say so many goodbyes—many of them sudden, as crises have sent so many people home (brain cancer in the family, an aging parent needing to go on dialysis, TB of the brain, and immigration visa disasters). We are so grateful for each teammate who has journeyed with us, for whatever length of time, and over the years, the Lord has taught me that we are called *to serve the people here*—not to a specific team. Teams may fall apart, but the people we are called to serve remain.

During the four months that the school was closed in 2020, we decided to tear down and completely rebuild our house. We knew that if we were going to survive the coming rainy seasons, we needed to make some changes: elevate the house by a meter with truckloads of rubble, redesign the floor layout, and add insulation to the ceiling. But the process of tearing down our home, which held so many memories, was excruciating.

During this break, we also decided that when it was time to reopen House of Hope, we would enlist the help of women from the neighborhood, since no Christians were interested in joining our Servants team at the time. No one on our team has ever had a background in primary education anyway—we have all learned by doing, so we invited three moms to join our team as "teacher's aids." Because none of them had graduated from middle school or had any teaching experience, they were all hesitant at first, but they were willing to try. Soon, all three became an integral part of House of Hope as full teachers. It was beautiful to watch them grow in self-confidence in the classroom as they discovered that they were very capable of teaching children how to read, write, and do basic math. A few years prior, a friend paid for us to purchase the *Saya Suka Membaca*[2] ("I Like to Read") curriculum and for all the teachers to be trained in how to teach it. This curriculum has made it much easier to teach new teachers how to teach, and it has also given us great tools for helping children to become literate—and to love reading.

---

1 In the course of the Servant's Jakarta team history, teammates and interns have come from the Netherlands, New Zealand, Australia, England, the US, and Indonesia.

2 See *Saya Suka Membaca*, https://www.sayasukamembaca.org/en/.

A few months after reopening House of Hope, Yosiah went to the market one morning in September 2020 to buy our vegetables—and as he was on his way home, a neighbor stopped him and said, "The land behind your house is for sale. Are you interested?" We had been praying about this empty lot for four years, wondering if we should try to buy it to expand the school. When we'd inquired several years earlier, we'd been told that the land was not for sale. So when Yosiah got home from the market, we prayed again—and that afternoon, Yosiah paid the down payment.

> It was beautiful to watch them grow in self-confidence in the classroom as they discovered that they were very capable of teaching children how to read, write, and do basic math.

The following morning, Yosiah looked at his phone in surprise—we had just received a first-time donation from a church in the US, who had transferred the amount we had spent to buy the land (plus a little extra!) straight to our Indonesian bank account. They had not known about the land, as we had not told anyone yet. We continue to be extremely grateful and to praise God for this confirmation and provision, which enabled us to add two more classrooms and a covered playground to House of Hope.

Three of our neighbor men built a beautiful new building, and I will never forget the look on our students' faces as they came running into the new space with its bright yellow walls the week of Thanksgiving[3] 2020. We now have a growing team of teachers—Yosiah and myself, Indonesian teammates, Bible school interns, as well as three moms from the neighborhood—and over a hundred students a year. From a time of great scarcity, we have now grown into a place of abundance.

Over the past ten years, we have met hundreds of children, and each child is uniquely gifted in different ways. Some children have extra challenges, whether it is their parental situation, financial struggles, or a learning disability. While some are self-motivated and excel, others lack excitement about the learning process and drag their feet, complaining about every task. It is heartbreaking to see children drop out of kindergarten or the early years of elementary education. What will their lives hold if they do not go to school? The cycle of poverty so easily continues, as children get sucked

---

3 I recognize that November Thanksgiving is not celebrated by much of the world, including Indonesia. However, for me when "American Thanksgiving" rolls around each year it will serve as the anniversary of opening the new House of Hope building. And we are deeply grateful to God for providing this new space for our students.

into working as garbage scavengers, beggars, or *manusia silver*.[4] But many children are eager and love learning, and it is a joy to teach them.

One such student is Mia. Mia joined House of Hope as a three-year-old. She was tiny for her age, but quickly we could see that she was very smart. Three-year-olds joined school only for play, singing, and story time, but by the time she was four Mia was impatient to start joining the "real classes." Mia's dad works as a garbage collector, and her family has moved to different shacks around the community at least four times in as many years. Stability is hard for our friends here. Shacks change owners, and often renters move locations as relational or physical problems arise. When Mia's mother was pregnant with Mia's younger sister, the shack where they were living was often downwind from a trash burning site. Visiting her made my stomach clench, as smoke poured in her direction—*what was this doing to their lungs? To the lungs of the growing baby?*

But amidst the financial stress of surviving on one garbage-route salary,[5] Mia's parents prioritize her education. She learned to read at House of Hope, and when she entered elementary school she was at the top of her class. Mia continues to come to afternoon lessons today, now as a third-grade student. Her smile, her enthusiasm for learning, and her laughter are contagious. It is an honor to help children like her learn.

Other children are not so fortunate. Some parents are illiterate and cannot help at all with their child's schooling. Divorce all too often wreaks havoc on families, spinning children into education disaster as they move home to the village or get sent to live with grandma.[6] It is not uncommon for women to work overseas, leaving children to be raised by grandparents. Many families that we know have aunts, daughters, mothers, or sisters working in Saudi Arabia, Taiwan, Singapore, or Malaysia.

Even finishing elementary school often seems impossibly hard for our friends here, but we continue to believe that these beautiful children deserve a chance. And we try to celebrate each little victory—like Mia—which is *great* in the eyes of the Lord.

---

4 "Silver people" literally paint themselves silver using metallic paint and then stand at intersections, begging for money. It is heartbreaking for me to think about the long-term health implications, especially for young children.

5 While garbage collectors supposedly receive government minimum wage, in reality this is not the case. Many neighborhoods do not have government garbage collection, and it is up to the local authority to decide on the salary. Often one salary is split between two men, as they take shifts doing the route. In our experience talking with neighbors here, the current salary for garbage collectors is $70 a month. Many men hold two routes, and also supplement their income by gathering all the recycling from the trash they collect.

6 Divorce rates are alarmingly high amongst the Sundanese and Javanese people. Underage marriage may contribute to this cycle.

Chapter 17

When Breath Departs

Who executes justice for the oppressed;
who gives food to the hungry.
The LORD sets the prisoners free;
the LORD opens the eyes of the blind,
the LORD lifts up those who are bowed down;
the LORD loves the righteous.
The LORD watches over the strangers;
he upholds the orphan and the widow.
–Psalm 146:7–9a

"They don't care if we die," Ibu Gusti told me, referring to the government. She said it jokingly, but I knew she partly believed it to be true. It was June 2021, and the Delta strain of the coronavirus was slamming Indonesia.[1]

When COVID-19 entered our vocabulary in March 2020, I wondered what it would look like when it hit our neighborhood, since it attacks the lungs and respiratory system—just like TB. Though researchers around the world immediately began to seek an effective vaccine and good medical treatment for this new disease, which is killing both rich and poor, tuberculosis has been with humanity since before the time of Christ.

And even though TB has been around for thousands of years and kills more people than any other infectious disease,[2] modern medicine has not yet developed a competent vaccine[3]—possibly because it is largely a disease of the poor. Before moving to Indonesia, I had never met anyone who had been treated for tuberculosis, and so I thought it was a disease of the past—something I had read about in *Les Miserables*.[4]

But TB is still an everyday battle for people in the majority world,

---

1 See Rahma, "Strangers and Aliens, https://www.alifeoverseas.com/strangers-and-aliens-covid-in-the-slums/.

2 More than a quarter of the world's population is infected with TB, but 90 percent of that is latent TB, meaning the person is not actively sick, nor is the person contagious. But if someone with TB bacteria in their body gets sick with something else or becomes malnourished, they can become actively sick with the deadly disease.

3 The BCG vaccine that exists protects against brain TB, but not against pulmonary TB (of the lungs).

4 One of the main characters, Fantine, dies of TB.

Tuberculosis has been with humanity since before the time of Christ.

as the bacteria can live for years and years in dark, unventilated rooms. The dark, crowded, poorly ventilated homes in slums mean that tuberculosis can spread very easily, often infecting entire families. Those who become actively sick die a slow death, infecting dozens of others with the bacteria before it kills them. The standard medical treatment is a complicated six-month process involving a combination of four antibiotics, but this requires an initial (and costly) diagnosis (involving X-rays, blood tests, and sputum tests). With proper treatment, people can recover, but the strong antibiotics often have bad side-effects on adults, which lead many people to stop taking the medicines as soon as they begin to feel "better." But stopping treatment only makes TB stronger, and then it can come back as MDR: multi-drug-resistant TB. Routinely taking the six-month treatment is especially difficult for those struggling with poverty, as they often move frequently and lack the stability to finish the full round of antibiotics.[5] *Here in Indonesia, TB is more commonly referred to as "fleck," perhaps because chest X-rays reveal white flecks in the lungs, or perhaps it refers to the flecks of blood coughed up by infected people.*

We learned about TB the hard way. In our first year teaching at House of Hope, one of our students became very ill and we took her to a doctor. I remember Yosiah carrying her up the hospital stairs, as she was too weak to walk. After that initial student, over the years we helped dozens of children and adults get tested and begin TB treatment. We learned to test not only students, but also their entire families, as TB infects everyone, and children normally contract it from adults in their household. Our team itself was not immune to the TB bacteria, and one of our teammates and his son with TB, but thankfully both recovered. Most recently, another teammate developed brain TB,[6] and we are still praying for his recovery. In our conversations with our neighbors, every single family—without exception—knows someone who has died of TB.

So when COVID-19 finally arrived in our neighborhood, with all the fury of the Delta strain, we watched with baited breath to see what

---

5 For a fascinating account of one courageous woman's fight against TB read Rachel Pieh Jones, *Stronger Than Death: How Annalena Tonelli Defied Terror and Tuberculosis in the Horn of Africa.*

6 While TB is most famous for affecting the lungs, it can also impact many other areas of the body, including the bones, the skin, the lymph nodes, and the brain.

would happen. Everyone seemed to get sick; the ball field became the daily "sunning" spot for people to get their vitamin D. The very sick were carried out on mats, their loved ones praying that the sunshine would drive the virus away. No one got tested. No one admitted they had the dreaded coronavirus. But all the symptoms were there, and when everyone on our team got sick, PCR swabs revealed that we were indeed positive. Thankfully, our whole team recovered, along with most of our neighbors. Others did not. No one had the privilege yet of getting a vaccine. No one had homes large enough to "self-isolate." Many of our friends and neighbors lacked the necessary government ID cards to go to the hospital if their sickness worsened. And the hospitals were overflowing anyway—and our neighbors had no interest in going there.

Perhaps in some small way, the COVID-19 pandemic allowed wealthier people to get a glimpse of the "normal" uncertainties and vulnerabilities in poorer communities. Even though we try to believe that we have life under control and that money can fix everything, when pandemics hit, we realize that at the end of the day, we are only vulnerable humans, and we are relying on broken bodies to keep us alive. We are all susceptible to coronavirus, TB bacteria, and a whole parade of other diseases.

In the midst of our COVID-19 isolation, my friend Mama Yani gave birth to her third child. We had known Mama Yani's family for years, as Yani had been one of our students. While pregnant, Mama Yani attended prenatal group faithfully each week. Her baby, Siti, was born more than a month early, and I was looking forward to finishing quarantine so I could visit. Her sixteen-year-old daughter-in-law had also given birth to a baby girl only a few weeks earlier. Their large household barely survived off the money made by Yani's father and older brother, who scavenged for recycling.

Two weeks after baby Siti was born, we were COVID-19 free and could start interacting with neighbors again. I was glad to sit outside on a plastic tarp on the ground and talk with Mama Yani. She was extremely pale and looked exhausted, and she told me she was recovering from being sick. I held swaddled baby Siti, who was so tiny, her poor body wracked by fits of coughing. Her mouth was full of white thrush patches, and she refused to nurse.

"Dear Lord," I prayed as I sat there, "Please do not let this baby die— especially while I am holding her!"

As we sat on the tarp, listening to the wailing of ambulances in the distance, I wondered what story about Jesus would be appropriate for this situation. Mama Yani had studied Scripture with me before, and I had prayed with her in the past. I felt stirred to share about how Jesus said, "Come to me, all you who are weary and carrying heavy burdens, and I will give you rest."[7] So I shared with her that Jesus understands suffering and is with us when we suffer. My heart ached for Mama Yani to know the love and care of our suffering savior, and I silently prayed, *Lord, protect your most vulnerable. Have mercy on those who are sick—with COVID-19 or TB or other diseases. Come heal our bodies. Come heal our souls. Come, Lord Jesus, come.*

> Jesus understands suffering and is with us when we suffer.

---

7 Matthew 11:28.

Chapter 18

Not Perfect, but Beautiful

"Aslan is a lion—the Lion, the great Lion."
"Ooh," said Susan. "I'd thought he was a man.
Is he—quite safe? I shall feel rather nervous
about meeting a lion." … "Safe?" said Mr. Beaver. …
"Who said anything about safe? 'Course he isn't safe.
But he's good. He's the King, I tell you."
–C. S. Lewis[1]

Not everything is hard and sorrowful in a slum. There are also beautiful moments when we get glimpses of the kingdom breaking in and we taste the indelible sweetness of getting to love our Master here. If we are following Jesus, there will be hard times—but there will be "overweights of joy"[2] along the way, too.

Children, of course, always help us not to take ourselves too seriously. Our own children and the neighborhood children help us to laugh, play, and remember to have fun each day. Every afternoon, the field near our house is a gathering place—a swimming pool during flooding months and the center of play during dry months, with pickup soccer games and sometimes organized leagues with everyone wearing uniforms. Girls play a game that is similar to jump rope—but made with rubber bands strung together. Kids stack their sandals together and play a tag game similar to "kick-the-can." When the coronavirus pandemic began, people in our neighborhood paid little attention to masks or social distancing—but on the field, children quickly invented a group tag game, yelling, "Corona! Corona!"

Our own sons have taught us a lot in this field—the joy of finding innumerable plastic straws, which can be used for all sorts of games. We each hold a straw and pull—and the straw that breaks first loses. Straws can be folded and made into all sorts of shapes, and they can be used for "drawing" pictures on the field. Our littlest son also finds "tiny treasures" in the field—broken toys, plastic bottle caps, and little "flowers."

---

1 Dorsett, *The Essential C. S. Lewis*, 93.

2 This phrase is from Amy Carmichael, *Overweights of Joy*.

He brings them home, gives the treasures a bath, and adds them to his toys. My children remind me that if we take the time to look for treasure, we will find it—and simple, ordinary things can bring us great joy, for happiness cannot be bought with money.

In the Gospel of Luke, Jesus tells us how to throw a party:

> When you give a luncheon or a dinner, do not invite your friends or your brothers or your relatives or rich neighbors, in case they may invite you in return, and you would be repaid. But when you give a banquet, invite the poor, the crippled, the lame, and the blind. And you will be blessed, because they cannot repay you, for you will be repaid at the resurrection of the righteous. (Luke 14:12–14)

My first experiment of trying to live out this Scripture was for my twentieth birthday in 2008. My brother and I decided to have a joint birthday party at the community center in Virginia where I had spent the summer interning, and so I felt known and loved there. We had a beautiful birthday party on the lawn, and our friends and guests were people struggling with homelessness, addiction, and poverty. The food was a conglomerate mix of potluck desserts and whatever food was donated that day.

Over the years, I have continued to find much joy in trying to implement Jesus's party instructions. For our sons' birthdays, we often choose to surprise our students with a party. We play games (pin the tail on the zebra, homemade piñatas, etc.), sing songs, and eat special food. If it is a surprise, then the children do not feel obliged to bring presents (and those who want to give presents can give them on another day). We do not want people to feel left out because they do not have money to buy a present. The presents that our sons do receive are often precious and beautifully wrapped: bars of soap, bottles of baby powder, flip flops, new underwear.

I remember my first birthday in Indonesia in 2011. I got up before dawn and went with my teammate Lisa (who was gracious enough to accompany me on my quest) to try to see the sunrise. We sat on the field filled with trash on the edge of our slum community and waited for the sun to rise. Since we are so near the equator, sunrises and sunsets are speedy things here—not the slow, drawn-out presentations I was used to in the States. But as I sat with Lisa, listening to the sound of chickens and the megacity waking up and swatting mosquitoes that were attacking us, I was overwhelmed with the beauty. The sight was

> My children remind me that if we take the time to look for treasure, we will find it

not perfect, but it was beautiful. This is the continual invitation in my life here—not to seek perfection, but to find the beauty. If you can look past the trash, ignore the smells, and tune out the noise—there is abundant beauty all around us, just waiting to be discovered.

I had a dream during my first year in Indonesia that someone was sending me and a friend on a mission—to hell—by way of a metro train. Our mission was simple: go visit the people there and tell them that the last train to leave would be at 4 p.m.

We arrived, got down from the train, and entered a prison schoolroom. We were underground, and the only light came from fluorescent light bulbs hanging from the ceiling. Everything was dreary and grey—no flames, no screaming, no apparent torture—but there were hundreds of men and women sitting in straight rows, with a woman teacher up front. When she saw us, she knew we had a message to share that she did not want her students to hear, so she continued with her lesson in a loud, monotone voice. Her teaching surprised me, as it was all about the rules the students had to follow in order to be "good" and "religious." The students just sat there with blank stares on their faces as the teacher/prison guard droned on and on.

> This is the continual invitation in my life here—not to seek perfection, but to find the beauty.

Then I started teaching, telling them about the grace of God and how Christ had been crucified to pay for their sins. I said there was no way that obeying all these rules would make them acceptable to God, but that Christ was offering them his unconditional love and acceptance. I told them that the train was leaving at 4 p.m., and they were all welcome to get on the train with me and leave this awful place.

Though we were underground, there was a window on the wall that looked into another world—heaven maybe. On the other side of the glass, you could see green grass, blue sky, and trees swaying in a gentle breeze. Inside the prison room, the air was stale, and the light was fake, but the sunshine, bright colors, and fresh air on the other side of the glass breathed *life* at me. Four o'clock could not come fast enough, and I wanted out of hell—right now! Sure enough, the train came right on time, and to my delight, lots of people lined up to get on. They grew suddenly excited as they realized that they were allowed to leave. The teacher was clearly mad, but could not stop them. Each person could choose for themselves where they wanted to be.

My friend commented as we were riding up and away from hell that it had not been such a bad place, after all. Perhaps she would come back someday—it seemed safe enough. I was flabbergasted by this. "How could you want to be somewhere so un-alive?" I asked, for that was the feeling of the whole place. Not suffering. Not torture. Not red-hot flames. Not death. But even worse—un-life. People who were content *not* to live, but to listen to a monotone voice droning on for eternity. People who could look out a window and glimpse the light and color and life that could be theirs, but did not want it. They were content to sit in a grey world.

While this was only a dream, it was intensely vivid and has stayed with me over the years. I do not want to be one of the people sitting in a grey world, afraid to live. Jesus promises that he has come to give us *abundant life* (John 10:10). And I am continually discovering that following Jesus is, indeed, life in abundance—whether it is laughing with my children as we play on the field, or throwing birthday parties with guests who will never invite us in return, or eating potluck meals with friends who are struggling with addiction. As I follow Jesus, my task is to invite others to join the party of life, too—both the Christians sitting next to me in church and my Muslim neighbors. Jesus wants us all to choose abundant life in him.

Chapter 19

According to What One Has

For if the eagerness is there, the gift is acceptable according to what one has—not according to what one does not have.
–2 Corinthians 8:12

"Here. Please take this," Grandma Sara said as she pressed two crumpled bills into my hands. Though we have always offered House of Hope lessons for free, in 2021 we talked with parents about putting a wooden box in front of the school for donations so that people could contribute to the work, if desired. Before we even bought the donation box, Grandma Sara pressed money into my hands.

Grandma Sara is raising her two grandchildren, as the parents are still teenagers themselves and are struggling with drug addiction. Grandma Sara cannot read or write, and so she takes great pride in the fact that her granddaughter is learning to read. The two bills she gave me are only worth fifteen cents—but in God's economy, I know they are priceless. Grandma Sara barely has enough food for herself and her grandchildren, but she wanted to offer what she could, giving us a gift that was acceptable *according to what she has*—rather than what she does not have (2 Cor 8:12).

When there is a crisis in the community—such as a hospitalization or death—people walk around the neighborhood with a cardboard box, collecting donations to help the struggling family. Similarly, when there is a celebration—circumcision parties, a baby's first steps, a girl's first menstruation, weddings, and first pregnancies—the community comes together to cook and share special food.

During first pregnancies, women celebrate *tujuh bulanan* ("the seventh month"). The woman and her family make a special spicy fruit salad with seven different fruits to give out to neighbors. The neighbors then bathe the woman with water (taken from seven different water sources) containing seven different types of flowers. This all happens on the 7th, 17th, or 27th of the month. When there is a death, the family members and close neighbors gather to bathe the body with flower water. From pregnancy to death, the community envelops everyone in the cycle of life. As our neighbors graciously welcome us into their lives—their celebrations as well as their times of mourning—they teach me about generosity and hospitality.

Throughout my life, I have reflected on what I am doing with all that I have been given—especially my education and wealth (compared to the majority of the world). How will I choose to share what has been entrusted to me? What will I do with my knowledge of Jesus, Scripture, and the gospel? These questions stirred me to move into a slum in Indonesia, and I am still trying to answer them each day through my life—in joyful thanksgiving for all that the Lord has given to me.

As I was writing this book, I got a cold and lost my voice for three days. I had not been yelling or leading people in worship or anything out of the ordinary, but suddenly I could only whisper. Losing my voice made me appreciate how much I rely on my voice throughout the day as I teach students, talk with my children, and sing worship songs. I also realized that what often comes out of my mouth is not something positive but negative—getting angry with my children or using a disappointed voice with students. When I could only whisper, I was reminded of the tongue's power to wound or to heal.

> I can unclench my hands, because *everything* belongs to the Lord.

When my voice finally returned, I realized that I am often too busy or distracted by the noise around me to hear God's voice. Each day, I can either decide to crowd my thoughts, schedule, and mind with noisy distractions—or I can choose to make room to listen to God, who is always speaking, always inviting me to hold my life, possessions, ministry, and family with open hands. I can unclench my hands, because *everything* belongs to the Lord.

As I reflected on these days of "muteness," I remembered another time I lost my voice—at the 2009 Urbana Missions Convention during my senior year of university, a season when I was wrestling with my calling to the slums. Though I sensed God inviting me to join Servants to Asia's Urban Poor after graduation, I was in a serious dating relationship at the time and did not know how my relationship could fit into my calling. I went to Urbana, longing for clarity and excited to reconnect with friends I had met during my previous summer doing the Global Urban Trek in Manila. But as soon as I arrived at Urbana, my voice disappeared—for the entire week. Because I could only whisper while gathering in a convention hall with 20,000 other college students, I could never be heard. I had been looking forward to worshiping with so many other students, but God seemed to be inviting me to listen and to raise my heart to him—rather than raising my voice.

On the last evening of the convention, we were gathered in the large worship hall, and I realized that I had forgotten my journal—which documented my entire previous year, including my trip to the Manila slums. Assuming I had left it in a seminar room earlier that evening, I ran through the convention center until I found the room. The lights were out, and so I had to make my way through the dark until I found the row of chairs where I had been sitting. When I finally found my journal, I breathed a deep sigh of relief—and then turned around and rushed back towards the main hall so that I could join the closing worship service. But then I saw Craig Greenfield, one of the international leaders of Servants at that time, sitting on the floor in a hallway, typing on his laptop. I had enjoyed listening to his seminars about Servants at Urbana and had been moved by his book about working with orphans in the slums of Phnom Penh, Cambodia,[1] and so I approached Craig and asked (in a whisper) if we could talk.

I sat down and explained that I felt called to Servants but was unsure about leaving my boyfriend, who was an amazing Christian young man. Craig listened and then said something I will never forget: "One of the main reasons people never end up on the mission field is because their spouse does not share the same calling." I knew I had to decide if I wanted to follow my personal desires or say "yes" to the Lord's invitation.

When I left Urbana, I knew what I had to do—but what I did not know was that exactly during that time, on the other side of the world, the Servants team was moving into the first slum community in Jakarta, and the team was desperately praying for another single female to join them. More than a year later, when I listened to Lisa, my first roommate in Jakarta, share about her prayers during that season, I realized that the Lord had been working in mysterious ways, indeed—all the way around the world.

Now, almost twelve years have passed, and as I watch my two beautiful children play and listen to the sounds of the students coming from House of Hope next door, I am so grateful that I lost my voice that week. For the Lord had a different plan than I could have imagined—to join me with Yosiah so that we could serve together in this slum. The Lord has been with me—and Yosiah and our children—through all the heartaches, tears, fires, floods, sicknesses, hospitalizations, learning, and struggles. As we continue this journey, we still have so much to learn from our Lord and our neighbors. Though there will continue to be pain, I *know* there will also continue to be so much joy.

---

1 Greenfield, *Urban Halo*.

> Though there will continue to be pain, I *know* there will also continue to be so much joy.

Chapter 20

My Daily Walk ... Home

*Without a deep confidence to cross barriers Christians will
simply not go to slums ... New kinds of Christian activists
are needed; activists motivated by the Spirit and by a sense
of call to move their lives to slums and to find ways to
adapt to the conditions.*
—*Ash Baker*[1]

A few mornings a week, I say goodbye to my boys and unlock our front door to step outside. It is early, and the sun's rays are gently warming up for a hot and humid day ahead. I sit down on the tiled porch and put my shoes on.

Across the street, Ibu Rosi is busy selling yellow rice, a common breakfast in Indonesia. My boys already bought their bowls of rice, tempeh, and *krupuk* (crackers) half an hour ago. We are often the first customers of the day for Ibu Rosi. In about an hour, she will tie a large basket laden with yellow rice and all the accompanying side-dishes on her back and walk around the neighborhood, selling it. Her husband became very sick with tuberculosis a few years ago and had to quit his job as a *bajaj* driver (motorcycle with sidecar). Though he eventually recovered from TB, he never went back to work, so Ibu Rosi has to support the family.

I wave to Mas Abal—our oldest son's best friend, whose family lives right in front of us—who is sitting on the bench outside his house. His mother passed away a year ago from uncontrolled diabetes. His eldest sister Siti, who graduated from hair salon school, keeps the family afloat.

Once my shoes are on, I start walking, greeting little Soleh, who is always barefoot. He has been walking since he was eight-months-old, and all the adults in his life struggle to keep up with him. He is being raised by his grandmother, although she calls him her son.

I continue walking and pass the group of garbage scavengers who live right behind our house. This morning, my five-year-old student, Andi, greets me, calling out, "*Kak* Anita!" It is clear he just woke up. His mom is hanging up laundry and asks the typical Indonesian greeting, "*Mau ke mana?*" ("Where are you going?"), even though she knows the answer.

---

1 Baker, *Slum Life Rising.*

I also pass several chickens, who are pecking at rice someone has thrown on a dry patch of the road. They avoid the mud puddles, just like I do. Several pigeons are also pecking at the ground, and one surprises me as it flies up right in front of me.

I pass a house that recently had yellow flags hanging in front of it, to let the neighborhood know that the woman who lived there had passed away. Her husband's motorcycle is parked out front, and I wonder how he is handling things.

On my right, I pass another student's small house, where Rani lives with his grandmother, grandfather, parents, and uncle's family. Rani's father and uncle both make a living selling fried snacks. When I pass them every morning, they are busy frying sweet potatoes, tempeh, tofu, and corn fritters. Rani's two-year-old cousin, who has been afflicted with awful boils, is on her mother's lap. As I pass, I notice a new boil forming on her nose and see the place her head has been shaved, where another boil is healing. She smiles, and I return the smile.

I stop in front of another former student's house because the mother, Mama Ria, is outside, sweeping her porch. I inquire about her eldest daughter, Marina, who got married at age thirteen to a twenty-some-year-old instead of entering middle school. After two years, Mama Ria tells me, Marina is "finally" pregnant. I ask Mama Ria when Marina plans to return from the village, where she and her husband are helping his family harvest the rice paddies. "After the harvest," she tells me. I tell Mama Ria about the Tuesday pregnancy group, and she promises to tell Marina to join us.

As I continue walking, I pass a number of men who are sleeping on benches or tables. I am guessing they were up late drinking, and decided not to return to their tiny houses with too many bodies and no air circulation. Sleeping outside doesn't seem like such a bad idea, but I wonder how they can sleep through the mosquito bites.

A motorcycle passes me with a cage full of tiny owls strapped to the back—most likely some new money-making scheme for our neighbors: raising and selling miniature owls.

I walk carefully around the last muddy section of the road and finally hit pavement as the road leads up and out of the slum. After a couple more minutes, I can finally start running—then have to stop at the large intersection and thread my way carefully across the busy road, which has no stop lights or crossing guards. After crossing the Sea of Cars, I start jogging again until I come to the gates of an upper-class community, where the security guards always smile and say, "Good morning," often in English.

I have entered another world, where servants are busy washing new cars, sweeping the pine needles off the street, or heading out to shop for the day's meals. In this neighborhood, the cobblestone roads are wide, so very different from the narrow, muddy streets I have just walked, which are always cluttered with motorcycles, laundry, trash, recycling, and children's broken (but usable) riding toys. Here, I do not know anyone's name, and no one knows mine.

I always notice a particular mansion with a front entryway that has an ornate ceiling fan. I can't help but wonder how much the fan cost or what purpose it serves, since no one would ever sit on that front entryway. I think of my neighbors, who have broken fans without covers to cool their tiny homes. I also pass three tennis courts, a man hitting golf balls into a net, a badminton court, and many other people walking or jogging through the neighborhood, along with countless cats.

After running for twenty minutes, I retrace my steps—say goodbye to the security guards, cross the Sea of Cars, descend into the muddy roads of the slum, and greet the same people. But now, instead of asking, "Anita, where are you going," they say, "Are you done already, Anita?" In this place, I am known by so many precious people, and I am so grateful to know each one.

> In this place, I am known by so many precious people, and I am so grateful to know each one.

In the half an hour that I have been gone, the neighborhood has continued to wake up. More children are in the streets, clutching small cash to go buy their first sugary junk of the day. Older siblings dressed in school uniforms are leaving by foot, bicycle, or motorcycle. Moms are feeding children, doing laundry, and cooking.

An elderly man returns with his garbage scavenging bag, which weighs heavily on his shoulder. I see him every day—sometimes on the streets picking up recycling, and sometimes back in the shacks behind our house. His thin body probably looks older than his actual age. He does not have a wife or children, and I often wonder what he thinks about as he sorts through his findings.

I look at the field by our house and see the muddy patches from too many soccer games, but I also see the sheep starting to graze in the long grass along the edges. Today, there are some new lambs, fresh and white, standing beside the ewes. It will not take long before the white wool fades into dirty grey and brown; but for a few weeks, we get to see the juxtaposition of snow-white lambs picking through colorful piles of plastic trash.

I turn left onto our street. When I reach our house, I take off my muddy shoes, place them back on the wooden beam above our porch, and call out, *"I'm home."*

Epilogue

For now we see only a reflection as in a mirror;
then we shall see face to face. Now I know in part;
then I shall know fully, even as I am fully known.
And now these three remain: faith, hope, and love.
But the greatest of these is love.
—1 Corinthians 13:12–13 NIV

The day after the fire in the slum community where I lived when I first moved to Jakarta in 2011, I traveled by public transportation across the city to meet a friend from my time with Servants in Vancouver, who was coming to visit. She now worked on a cruise ship and was going to be in Jakarta for an afternoon. The timing was unfortunate, as the trauma from the fire the night before was still fresh, but I had been looking forward to this day for weeks and had promised to pick my friend up and bring her to the slum for the day.

When I got to the docks, I found myself standing with a bunch of Indonesians who were waiting to greet loved ones who worked on the ship and give them home-cooked meals and other care packages. The ship was running late, and we had to wait for two hours for the ship to dock. When it finally arrived, a parade of foreigners disembarked—and then got on air-conditioned buses that would take them to a nearby mall for the day. It was surreal to watch so many tan, scantily clad bules walk down the gangplank. I remember some of the Indonesians who were standing there waiting, *clapping* as all the foreigners walked by.

Once all the tourists had departed, my friend was finally allowed to get off and come with me to the slum, where we walked by the ruins of the fire to my house and had an encouraging time of praying and worshipping together. A few hours later, we returned to the ship docks, where we sat together and talked as we waited for the call to return to the ship.

"Not every follower of Christ is called to the slums," she commented.

"But I have to believe that more people are called," I said. "God has not forgotten the slums. Surely, God desires more of his followers to serve him in poor communities."

The air-conditioned buses soon returned to the docks, and the tourists reboarded the ship, carrying

God has not forgotten the slums.

packages and bags stuffed with the things they had purchased at the mall. Having "experienced" Jakarta, they were now continuing their cruise. I hugged my friend goodbye, and watched as she disappeared into the ship.

~⌐

In writing this book, my hope has been to give readers—who may never step into a slum—a glimpse of Jakarta beyond its malls and shopping districts, beyond the walls of its gated communities and tall glass buildings. I am trying to use my voice to express what I have seen and heard in this particular city, in the particular slum where I live. I wish that you could come and sit with my neighbors and listen to their stories firsthand, for they have beautiful voices and have taught me so much. I hope that these stories have helped you come to know these neighbors as individual people with unique histories, faces, and interests—they are more than a statistic.

I also hope that my account has given you a glimpse into the beautiful adventure of following Christ, even when it means digging through the thick walls that separate us from our neighbors who are living in an urban slum on the other side of the world. Perhaps some of you will choose to give a few years of your life to loving Jesus in slum communities. Perhaps some of you will be moved to support this work financially and pray for those who are sent. Or if you are already digging through walls to follow Jesus into difficult places, I hope these words will encourage you to keep following Jesus—and falling in love with him—as you trust that he is *with* you and will never abandon you.

I hope these words will encourage you to keep following Jesus—and falling in love with him—as you trust that he is with you and will never abandon you.

Freedom Rains [1]

Rain falls lightly, drizzling its prayer for life
Over this concrete wilderness, where grass garden picnics scream,
SUBVERT, over the din of dealing whispers—"Upper, Downer."
Amidst traffic and footsteps,
the fragrance of incense
replaces the ever-present pot cloud.
Rain falls gently, and I wonder at its patience.
Floodgates, let forth! Be freed!
Like my friend's repressed tears.
I see her silenced agony, her blinking eyes.
Speaking as if she cannot hear herself,
cannot feel the words on her tongue.
From brain to voice, does it miss the heart?
In her ocean of pain,
I want to reclaim lament, my humanity, her childhood.
Damn the wolves in sheepskins!
The One who died on the cross
does not sanction genocide, apartheid, or suburban white fences.
Behind our barrier walls of fear and distance,
we are each trapped in self-made prisons.
Freedom come. Freedom breathe. Freedom rain.

---

1 Written during my time in the Downtown Eastside of Vancouver, BC. July 2010.

Your Body [2]

Your Body is broken, Lord. Dividing over how to sing songs, what color carpets to have, or whether Styrofoam cups should be used during fellowship time. Splintered into cliques bearing the names of leaders instead of Yours. Causing confusion to the world. Where is the unity in the Body? Eyes are trying to walk. Hands try to sing. Kneecaps want to be elbows. And sick with the disease of complacency. Disciples turning into bench warmers, carrying Your name but not following You to the cross. Is there a cure?

This is Your Body, and I am called to love You.

Your Body is broken, Lord. On street corners, holding out Your hand to receive small change from those who pass by without seeing. You are the children who board buses, playing small guitars and bellowing out songs. You are plagued with scabies—scratched open sores bleeding. Itching all night long. You are sick with TB, with measles, with sleepless nights and tired days. You drop out of elementary school. Your head has lice and You've worked overseas in Saudi Arabia. Your thin hair reveals malnutrition.

Your Body is oh so broken, Lord, and sometimes painful to look at.
But I'm called to love you.

Your Body is broken, Lord. Sandaled feet tread many miles on rocky paths. Making Your way to Jerusalem 2000 years ago—in a time of Roman Empire oppression and rumblings of rebellion. Your feet and hands nailed to rough wood. Your head adorned with thorns cruelly twisted for your crown. Your side pierced. Your blood mingling with the tears of Your followers.

Your Body is broken, Lord, declaring Your love.

Your Body is broken, Lord. Wheat of the field winnowed and ground. Smashed to pieces to create flour—kneaded into bread. Broken in order to share. The cup of wine—grapes also pressed down, crushed. Passed from one thirsty soul to another.

Your Body is broken, Lord, and we thank You.

And in the midst of this brokenness, You declare resurrection. The wounds will one day only be scars. The tomb is empty. The poor hear good news. The cup is the New Covenant.

---

2 Written in Jakarta, July 4, 2011

Naming Orchids [3]

Created in God's image
To love, to bless, to serve,
Instructed to plant seeds with sweat and toil
What has become of humanity?
Incubating in test-tubes,
Flowers to name after the rich and famous.
While in hidden rooms imported maids slave away
And the wealthy pay exorbitant fees to have a car.
Skinny children drop out of primary school,
Lacking $15 uniform fees
And salads are eaten by self-starved models
For that price.
Insanity becomes normal in this globalized world,
Where most are blind to their neighbors,
Reaching out hands that each day are still empty.
Don't forget the stable-born Nazarene,
Who proclaimed simple lilies
Teach all of God's provision.
The pillowless One,
Come to fill the empty and
Topple the powerful.
When the orchid-named celebrities
May be left confused at their worthless billions—
While the slum children rejoice in the
Feast of the Kingdom.

---

3 On a "visa-run" to Singapore in 2011, I visited an orchid park, where celebrities can indeed have orchids named after them.

Words of Peace[4]

Jesus, be the air I breathe
The smoke envelops, and threatens to engulf me.
Jesus, be the light I need.
I can't see the way to walk in this darkness.

>I find myself in this boat again,
>The wind and waves surround me.
>I know You're Lord of Heaven and earth.
>Won't you speak Your words of peace?

Jesus, be the hope I need.
Despair surrounds me, and threatens to drown me.
Jesus, be the Truth I need.
Dispel the lies, replace them with Your Spirit.

>I find myself in this boat again,
>The wind and waves surround me.
>I know You're Lord of Heaven and earth.
>Won't you speak Your words of peace?

"The LORD, Your God, is with you.
He is mighty to save.
He will take great joy in you.
He will quiet you with his love.
He will rejoice over you with singing."[5] Alleluia.

>I find myself in this boat again,
>Awake, arise, and save me.
>I know You're Lord of Heaven and earth.
>Thank You for Your words of peace.
>You are the Word of Peace.

---

4 A song written during the COVID-19 pandemic, June 2020.
5 An adaption of Zechariah 3:17.

Acknowledgments

I had no intention of writing a book—at least, not for another decade or so. But I am deeply grateful to my parents for encouraging me to write now and not wait. "Write the book while the memories are fresh," my dad told me one day over a video call. Thank you, Mom and Dad, for believing that my story was worth sharing. Thank you for your love and support over all these years. Thank you for reading the initial manuscript and offering valuable comments and questions.

Thank you to Jason and Laura Porterfield for your obedience to God's call to start the Servant's to Asia's Urban Poor Jakarta team so many years ago. Thank you for your continued prayers and support—even from afar. Thank you, Jason, for believing in this book project and answering many questions along the way.

I am also deeply grateful to Elizabeth Trotter, editor-in-chief of A Life Overseas blog. Thank you for publishing my first articles, providing me with encouragement, and saying that my voice needed to be heard. Thank you for answering countless emails and questions regarding the publishing process.

I am forever grateful for my sending church family. Your prayers, your support, your songs, and your friendships have carried me through some of the darkest and most beautiful times of my life. Although you are a tiny church rooted in Virginia, the ripples of your faithfulness and love continue to impact me across the ocean. And a special thanks to those who have served on our ministry support team, praying for us loyally all these years.

Thank you to all those who read different versions of this manuscript-in-process and offered valuable feedback: Stephanie, Craig, Mary, Lucas, Katie, Irene, Caroline, Mark, Bob, and others.

This book would not be what it is without the masterful editing of Karen Hollenbeck. Thank you for taking this project on. Thank you for hearing the heart of the stories.

Thank you to my friend Fadli for creating such a wonderful cover design. And thank you to the editors at William Carey Publishing for believing in this book.

And a big thank you to my team here in the slum community. Thank you for supporting me in this time-consuming endeavor.

Thank you to my husband, Yosiah, for freeing me to write. Thank you for believing in me even when I struggle to do so. Following Jesus together with you over these past ten years has been the most beautiful adventure. Thank you for your courage, your laughter, and your love. Thank you to our two sons for putting up with all these months of mommy typing. You two did not choose this story, but I trust that it is not by accident that the Lord entrusted you to our family. Thank you for seeing it as an adventure too.

And thank you to the hundreds of gracious Indonesians who have welcomed me into your homes, your hearts, and your lives. Thank you for being my teachers. This book would not exist without you.

Baker, Ash. *Slum Life Rising: How to Enflesh Hope within a New Urban World*. Birmingham, UK: Urban Shalom Publishing, 2012.

Bessenecker, Scott. *Living Mission: The Vision and Voices of the New Friars*. Downers Grove: InterVarsity, 2010.

Bessenecker, Scott. *The New Friars: The Emerging Movement Serving the World's Poor*. Downers Grove: InterVarsity, 2006.

Bonhoeffer, Dietrich. *Cost of Discipleship*. New York: Touchstone, 1959.

Brother Roger of Taize, *Parable of Community*. Oxford: Mowbray, 1980.

Carmichael, Amy. *Overweights of Joy* in *Amy Carmichael: Her Early Works* (13-in-1), Kindle ed. 2016.

Carmichael, Amy. *Edges of His Ways: Selections for Daily Readings*. Fort Washington, PA: CLC Publications, 1980.

DMM Frontier Missions. www.dmmfrontiermissions.com (November 17, 2021).

Dorsett, Lyle W. *The Essential C. S. Lewis*. New York: Scribner, 2017.

Duncan, Michael. *Costly Mission: Following Jesus into Neighborhoods Facing Poverty*. Melbourne, Australia: UNOH, 1996/2011.

Elliot, Elisabeth. *A Chance to Die: The Life and Legacy of Amy Carmichael*. Ada: Revell, 2005.

Fikkert, Brian, and Steve Corbett. *When Helping Hurts: How to Alleviate Poverty without Hurting the Poor … and Yourself*. Chicago: Moody, 2009.

Greenfield, Craig. *Urban Halo: Stories of Hope for Orphans of the Poor*. Milton Keynes, UK: Authentic Media, 2007.

Grigg, Viv. *Cry of the Urban Poor: Reaching the Slums of Today's Mega-Cities*. Milton Keynes, UK: Authentic Media, 1992.

Grigg, Viv. *Companion to the Poor: Christ in the Urban Slums*. Lafayette Hill, PA: Marc, 1990.

Hayes, John. "Incarnational Ministry Among the Poor." Servants Jakarta Information Pack, November 2008.

Hurnard, Hannah. *Hinds' Feet on High Places*. Nashville: Tyndale, 1955.

Jones, Rachel Pieh. *Stronger Than Death: How Annalena Tonelli Defied Terror and Tuberculosis in the Horn of Africa*. Walden, NY: Plough, 2019.

Joshua Project. "Sunda in Indonesia" (November 15, 2021). https://joshuaproject.net/people_groups/15121/ID.

Langberg, Diane. *Suffering and the Heart of God: How Trauma Destroys and Christ Restores*. Greensboro, NC: New Growth, 2015.

Myers, Bryant L. *Walking with the Poor: Principles and Practices of Transformational Development*. New York: Orbis, 2011.

Nyman, James. *Stubborn Perseverance*. Mt. Vernon: Mission Network, 2017.

Porterfield, Jason. "Three Characteristics of Pioneer Missionaries." Servants Jakarta Information Pack, November 2008.

Rahma, Anita. "Digging Through the Wall." A Life Overseas (January 4, 2022). https://www.alifeoverseas.com/digging-through-the-wall/.

Rahma, Anita. "Jesus Doesn't Want Our Used Underwear." Servants to Asia's Urban Poor (July 22, 2021). servantsasia.org/jesus-doesnt-want-our-used-underwear/.

Rahma, Anita. "Let Us Go to Him." Servants to Asia's Urban Poor (March 3, 2021). https://servantsasia.org/let-us-go-to-him/.

Rahma, Anita. "Strangers and Aliens: Covid in the Slums." A Life Overseas (July 26, 2021). https://www.alifeoverseas.com/strangers-and-aliens-covid-in-the-slums/.

Saya Suka Membaca. https://www.sayasukamembaca.org/en/ (April 20, 2022).

Travis, John. "The C1 to C6 Spectrum: A Practical Tool for Defining Six Types of 'Christ-Centered Communities' ('C') Found in the Muslim Context." *Evangelical Missions Quarterly* 34, no. 4 (1998): 407–8.

Trousdale, Jerry. *Miraculous Movements: How Hundreds of Thousands of Muslims Are Falling in Love with Jesus*. Nashville: Thomas Nelson, 2012.

Woodberry, Dudley. *From Seed to Fruit: Global Trends, Fruitful Practices, and Emerging Issues among Muslims*. Pasadena: William Carey Library, 2008.

Bessenecker, Scott. *Living Mission: The Vision and Voices of the New Friars*. Downers Grove: InterVarsity, 2010.

Bessenecker, Scott. *The New Friars: The Emerging Movement Serving the World's Poor*. Downers Grove: InterVarsity, 2006.

Carmichael, Amy. *Candles In the Dark: Letters of Amy Carmichael*. Fort Washington: CLC, 2012.

Carmichael, Amy. *God's Missionary*. Fort Washington: CLC, 1939/1997.

Carmichael, Amy. *Gold by Moonlight*. Fort Washington: CLC, 1935/2013.

Carmichael, Amy. *Gold Cord: The Story of a Fellowship*. Fort Washington: CLC, 1932/2002.

Carmichael, Amy. *If: What Do I Know of Calvary Love*. Fort Washington: CLC, 1938/2011.

Carmichael, Amy. *Mimosa: A True Story*. Fort Washington: CLC, 1924/2011.

Carmichael, Amy. *Ploughed Under: A Young Girl's Obedience. God's Ever-Present Grace*. Fort Washington: CLC, 1935/2013.

Carmichael, Amy. *Rose From Brier*. Fort Washington: CLC, 1933/2012.

Claiborne, Shane. *The Irresistible Revolution*. Grand Rapids: Zondervan, 2006.

Greenfield, Craig. *Subversive Jesus: An Adventure in Justice, Mercy, and Faithfulness in a Broken World*. Grand Rapids: Zondervan, 2016.

Jack, Kristin. *The Sound of Worlds Colliding: Stories of Radical Discipleship from Servants to Asia's Urban Poor*. Phnom Penh, Cambodia: Hawaii Printing House, 2009.

Jones, E. Stanley. *The Christ of the Indian Road*. Nashville: Abingdon, 1926.

Jones, E. Stanley. *The Unshakable Kingdom and the Unchanging Person*. Bellingham, WA: McNett, 1972/1995.

Jones, Rachel Pieh. *Pillars: How Muslim Friends Led Me Closer to Jesus*. Walden, NY: Plough, 2021.

Love, Rick. *Muslims, Magic and the Kingdom of God*. Pasadena: William Carey Publishing, 2000.

Mallouhi, Christine. *Miniskirts, Mothers, and Muslims: A Christian Woman in a Muslim Land*. Grand Rapids: Monarch, 2004.

Marrie, Jeanie. *Across the Street and Around the World: Following Jesus to the Nations in Your Neighborhood … and Beyond*. Nashville: Thomas Nelson, 2018.

Medearis, Carl. *Muslims, Christians, and Jesus: Gaining Understanding and Building Relationships*. Minneapolis: Bethany House, 2008.

Nouwen, Henri. *Can You Drink This Cup?* Notre Dame: Ave Maria, 2006.

Pullinger, Jackie. *Chasing the Dragon: One Woman's Struggle Against the Darkness of Hong Kong's Drug Dens*. Minneapolis: Chosen, 1980/2013.

Talman, Harley, and John Travis. *Understanding Insider Movements: Disciples of Jesus within Diverse Religious Communities*. Pasadena: William Carey Publishing, 2006.

InnerChange: www.innerchange.org

 MoveIn: www.movein.global

 Servants to Asia's Urban Poor: www.servantsasia.org

 Servant Partners: www.servantpartners.org

 Word Made Flesh: www.wordmadeflesh.org

Visit us at missionbooks.org

Beyond Poverty: Multiplying Sustainable Community Development

Terry Dalrymple, Author

Terry Dalrymple calls us to move beyond sustainable projects in a single village to transformational movements that multiply change from village to village and sweep the countryside. This book tells the story of a large and growing network of ministries around the world using the strategy of Community Health Evangelism.

Paperback & ePub

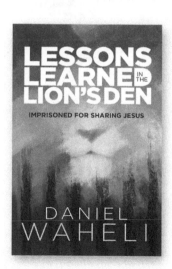

Lessons Learned in the Lion's Den: Imprisoned for Sharing Jesus

Daniel Waheli, Author

Lessons Learned in the Lion's Den shares the journey of one missionary family as the father is detained in a predominantly Muslim country in Africa. The accounts of his wife and two young children offer a glimpse into the inner life of the family during this trying time. The heart of this story is not a man imprisoned, but a family united—in hope, love, and a pressing desire that God be glorified in all things.

Paperback & ePub

WILLIAM CAREY PUBLISHING